G000081204

great

BRITISH FOOD

great
BRITISH
FOOD

HEATHER HAY FFRENCH

Quiller Press
London

1 London

2 Kent

3 South East

4 West Country

5 Hampshire & Cotswolds

6 Wales

7 Anglia

8 Middle England

9 Heart of England

10 Yorkshire

11 North West

12 Scotland

13 Northern Ireland

First published 2000 by Quiller Press Ltd, 46 Lillie Road, London, SW6 1TN

Copyright © 2000 Heather Hay Ffrench

ISBN 1 899163 56 5

Jacket by Pat McCreeth

Designed by Jo Lee

Printed in Hong Kong by Colorcraft Ltd.

No part of this publication may be reproduced in any way or by any means without the prior written permission of the publishers.

contents

foreword

by gordon summerfield • chairman • Food from Britain

Over the last few years, Modern British cooking has sparked a latent passion for food and drink throughout the United Kingdom.

As hungry consumers, we now avidly watch food and drink programmes featuring celebrity British chefs, read food and drink magazines and restaurant reviews in newspapers and spend more time browsing in the supermarkets picking out exciting new products to take home to cook.

It has also encouraged us to spend more of our leisure time dining out. In fact, British cuisine is now regarded as very much in vogue with many modern restaurants experimenting with infusing traditional British dishes with Mediterranean and Asian flavours.

Competition is nowhere more apparent than in the supermarkets, where on a daily basis the key players aim to win greater share of your custom. Manufacturers in turn have had to provide quality, innovation and variety second to none to meet the supermarkets' exacting requirements. In turn, this has made them a very attractive proposition for international supermarkets looking to source great British food.

Many of us are familiar with the big household brands but at the other end of the scale there are the less well known British Speciality food companies which are often rural based, farmhouse kitchen companies employing just a few people. Britain's superb range of Speciality food and drink products

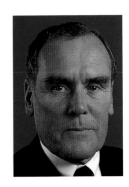

reflect the country's rich heritage and we as a nation are increasingly seeking out traditionally produced regional products via fine food outlets and in supermarket delicatessens.

We, as consumers, appreciate their single-minded dedication to quality, products achieved through care, craftsmanship and attention to ingredients and detail. Today, in the United Kingdom, you can find an array of traditional fare second to none. Other producers are spearheading a new wave of innovative products such as unusual or organically grown fruit and vegetables, salad dressings and sauces, continental-style smoked meats or fish, organic dairy products and special occasion cakes and biscuits.

Without a doubt these people are the seedcorn of our industry and some will be the big names of the future.

Food from Britain helps them develop their business whatever their future plans. Speciality companies can take advantage of business development services provided by a network of regional speciality groups set up by Food from Britain. When a company is ready to build international sales, Food from Britain has a host of services provided by its head office in London and its 12 international offices across Europe, North America and Japan to help grow overseas business.

As Chairman of Food from Britain, I am delighted to be sponsoring *Great British Food*. I hope you spend many happy hours finding the best of British food in our beautiful Isles.

Conversion tables

WEIGHTS	
oz	**g**
1/2	10
3/4	20
1	25
1 1/2	40
2	50
2 1/2	60
3	74
4	110
4 1/2	125
5	150
6	175
7	200
8	225
9	250
10	275
12	350
1lb	450
1lb 2oz	500
1lb 8oz	700
2	900
3	1.35kg

DIMENSIONS	
inch	**metric**
1/8	3mm
1/4	5
1/2	1cm
3/4	2
1	2.5
1 1/4	3
1 1/2	4
1 3/4	4.5
2	5
2 1/2	6
3	7.5
3 1/2	9
4	10
5	13
5 1/4	13.5
6	15
6 1/2	16
7	18
7 1/2	19
8	20
9	23
9 1/2	24
10	25.5
11	28
12	30

VOLUME	
1 fl oz	27.5 ml
2	55
3	75
5 (1/4 pt)	150
10 (1/2 pt)	275
1 pint	570
1 1/4	725
1 3/4	1 litre
2	1.2
2 1/2	1.5
4	2.25

OVEN TEMPERATURES		
Gas mark	**°F**	**°C**
1	275	140
2	300	150
3	325	170
4	350	180
5	375	190
6	400	200
7	425	220
8	450	230
9	475	240

author's preface

With regional specialities to buy, beautiful places to see, exciting places to eat and a multitude of new recipes to cook, I hope *Great British Food* provides a hamper you can enjoy for a long time. Being, inevitably, of a finite length, the following pages contain only some of the great variety of tastes available in Britain today. Fortunately, at the start of the new Millennium, the Internet provides a way to add more Great British Food; you can find it on www.greatbritishfood.co.uk. Another site www.foodfirst.co.uk has a full directory of UK specialist food producers with more recipes and up-to-the-minute food news. On the Food from Britain websites: www.foodfrombritain.com and ww.speciality-foods.com the organisation has launched a British Speciality shopping mall, so if you want samples or even do your own shopping, look them up on the website.

Metric units have been used throughout; there is a conversion table opposite if you would like to change them. All the recipes - unless otherwise stated - are for 4 persons.

My family makes preserves and confectionery; we have a small, regional business that is a member of Kentish Fare, an association of food producers. All over Britain such associations, under the guidance of Food from Britain, help companies develop and reach their marketplace. The regional groups are all listed at the back of the book and the chapters I have written reflect the areas they cover. Some, like the West Country, cover several counties while others, like the one for Kent, a single county.

About half of the photos in the book were taken to illustrate recipes and products in the text, the rest to bring additional products to your attention – and to help further exploration there is a directory of wine producers who welcome visitors, and a list of distilleries where you can see production methods and 'try and buy'. I've also included a personal list of places to shop, eat and visit to get a feel of the different tastes available around the country. The best way to appreciate our food is to eat it.

I would like to thank my family for putting up with the necessary domestic upheaval that writing *Great British Food* entailed. My children have been an invaluable help – they have delighted in discoverling new tastes and in reminding me of old favourites, Alex has been a major contributor to the photographs and Rex an important contributor to my spelling. Joanna and her husband David cook exciting modern dishes, their three small children enjoy colourful fresh food, and of course, tomato sauce! Jonathan, my husband, has been an enthusiastic researcher, cooking some and tasting all of the recipes – and finally I would like to thank my mother, for teaching me to cook in the first place and setting me off on what is a continual edible adventure.

introduction

What is Great British Food?

A lifetime of buying, cooking and eating 'British', and several years of specific research for this book have provided many answers.

Modern British cooking combines superlative quality ingredients with innovative, at times deceptively simple ways of cooking often influenced by foreign travel and always by design. Traditional British cooking is based on a wealth of culinary history – the great roasts of old England, fine game dishes from Scotland, Irish Stew scented with garden herbs, and inimitable Welsh lamb.

As for speciality produce, a new breed of food producer has developed out of our nation's delight in independence. Many good amateur cooks have turned their abilites to profit, become professional at producing jams or cakes or other delicious consumables that they once made only for pleasure.

There are large companies often grown from family enterprises that produce thousands of food items a day, all to exacting standards, and with a focus on the world-wide market.

Visiting the counties of Great Britain for research has been an edible adventure. Sometimes I was returning to places I had been before, but there were many new areas to discover, new views to see, and constantly new tastes to enjoy. My pursuit for edible delights brought me into contact with hundreds of enthusiastic professionals and I thank everyone who helped me with information and contributions – without them the book would be lifeless. Chefs and cooks, farmers and growers, producers of cheese, of preserves, bakers and millers, executives responsible for multi-million pound businesses based on forseeing future food fashions, and the lady who makes toffee like granny used to, in small pans, by the kilogram batch and sells it at a Farmers market – all gave their time and energy.

Some of the recipes were created by chefs, others by producers with passion for their product who have put time and care into devising recipes to display them at their best. All use British products at their best, seasonal and fresh. As a caterer I have had exciting opportunities to create dishes to show off fine British produce. Cooking for Orient Express Tours at Penshurst Place in Kent meant designing dishes that retained a real taste of Britain and appealed to international palates. Asked to cook olde English fruits for Carlton TV led me to make meddlar pies, quince soufflés and mulberry gin, and to learn that the Romans used quinces to scent the bathroom and that mulberry stains forever.

Leisure and pleasure food shopping is an excellent reason to visit new places. A weekend outing to the coast, to bring back fresh fish to enjoy and some to freeze for later. A pick-your-own afternoon in the strawberry fields provides the fruit and the appetite for summer treats.

My family enjoys cottage holidays renting somewhere we haven't been before, buying what is best in local food and drink – then having leisurely cook-ins, followed by delicious dinners. When we're tired or lazy we eat out – often choosing somewhere recommended by the cottage visitors book. We haven't yet chosen a cottage holiday specifically because of a restaurant review, but friends have – they went to Scotland to follow up a glowing magazine piece five years ago and go back every year because the food is so good. If I tend to eulogise about idyllic food, then I'm not forgetting all the hard work that went into preparing it. Food production and preparation requires a professional. There are agricultural colleges to serve all of Britain and there are chefs schools. Everyone concerned with the preparation of food in the UK must take hygiene courses. Many visitors to Britain's Tudor England were amazed by the quality of the meat. The fact that it could be served and enjoyed in great roasts was a sign of its quality. Today many visitors to Britain still expect to be served roast beef as our national dish, and they still can be, but they also have perhaps the widest choice on earth, because Britain welcomes new food and food styles, adapting and absorbing, creating trends and fashions and delighting in the use of the finest, freshest often home-grown ingredients.

Below: A composition of bread.

millennium

What do you think will be the future tastes of Britain?

I must have asked that question hundreds of times in the past few months and the answers have all led on to discussions on mealtimes - do families eat together anymore? Are we all going to eat out more and more? Truthfully, does anyone cook anymore, or do we just pop something tasty in the microwave and watch a chef cook up a brilliant meal on TV?

However, whatever and whenever we eat, one thing is certain, food is talked about more in Britain today than ever before, and tastes are changing, so what to? There must be clues in new shopping developments, such as Bluewater in Kent. Every fifty yards you'll be offered the chance to sit and enjoy a little light refreshment. It's shopping and grazing and the food that suits is quickly consumed - designer frothy coffee and a pain au chocolat or a burger and Coke. And the quality of goodies on offer in countrywide malls is increasing by the tried and tested route of customer selection. If we're bored with a presentation of uninspiring sandwiches, light on garnish, then we can shop with our feet and pass on to where there's a filled baguette, or toasted ciabatta, perhaps with a little smoked salmon, cream cheese, a touch of avocado?

Can you remember back to when the only pasta we ate was macaroni? Have you joined the happy band enjoying quick-cook couscous for a nourishing, very nearly instant meal?

Sammy's Summer Taboulé
Cooking time six minutes!

Make up 1 carton of couscous and cool. Finely chop the parsley and mint, cut the vegetables into small pieces and keep the juice. In a large bowl mix together all the ingredients with the couscous and olives. Chill in the fridge for 1 hour and stir again. Garnish with mint leaves.

**1 carton Sammy's Middle Eastern with pine nut and sultana couscous
1 large onion
300g green and black olives
Juice of 2 lemons
15g mint leaves (keep a few to garnish)
1 bunch of parsley
4floz glass olive oil
Salt and pepper**
Serves 6

Opposite: Shopping on-line, saving time, effort and energy to spend on leisure and pleasure shopping – on foot.

All recipes serve 4 unless otherwise stated

Opposite: Couscous: Wonderfully quick to prepare, delicious to eat as it is, or with an aromatic vegetable stir fry with fresh ginger and cool thick sheep's milk yoghurt.

The Great British Food revolution is being led by something that Britain has always been a world leader in - fashion. Just as passionate discussions are being held in the foody corridors of power about herbs and spices as were ever held in the 'rag-trade' about hem lengths.

I've just been to what might be termed 'foodie heaven', the world's largest trade food fair, Anuga in Cologne. Thousands of exhibitors – literally, with stand after glossy stand professionally decked to show off every edible delight you can imagine. And many are themed by nation, Spain a vibrant red, Italy Tuscany umber. The highly decorative wooden village that China had erected was complete with a scent of the Orient. Vast open freezers were piled high with milk-white frozen squid and octopus as round as pumpkins – Damien Hurst would have loved it. Fat sausages, thin sausages, and everywhere buyers and producers, looking, tasting, alert for trends, for keys to unlock their potential in the greatest marketplace on earth.

I was there to look at British exhibitors, to do a little tasting - wonderful! And a lot of talking - I talked so much I came home croaking, but there was so much to see. Forman's of Whitepost Lane, London, offered a tasting of their world renowned smoked salmons, from the farmed fish first, and then the wild - both so good, but oh the wild… Noon's, 'The World of Authentic Eastern Cuisine', from Middlesex, were serving hot curry all day, every day, for the week of the show and it was delicious, the rice fragrant and the curry fresh and spicy. A sip of Elderflower Pressé from Belvoir Cordials, a summer day in a glass. Everywhere a supreme professionalism and 'quality' the buzz word.

A kind of magic circle has been explained to me. With my husband, I run a small, specialist food production company. We make mustards and jams, we have done for a long time. Like many other small producers we enjoy what we do and do not want to make our company any bigger.

But if we were different, if we did want to expand and grow then we would enter the circle. Our first step would be to try and sell our products to the 'big boys', the supermarkets. And it has become a lot more feasible to take that step because many of the large chains are approaching small specialist producers, appreciating that an increasingly discerning marketplace wants to buy 'something different'. Having the supermarkets express interest in your product means that if you want to do business with them you have to change gear. To create a method of production that takes all your standards far beyond the law of the land, and to maintain that level continually, to be aware that the ultra rigid regulations of Marks and Spencers, of Sainsburys, of Safeways and many others are being applied to you and your products. The result is dynamic. The passion of small enterprise fused with the 'clout' of big business makes for superlative quality – and that's the supreme quality that Britain was 'showing off' in Cologne, combined with an innovative sense of food fashion. Future tastes of Britain - anything you can dream of and more!

Below: Just to prove that millennia may come and go, but oysters will be popular for ever.

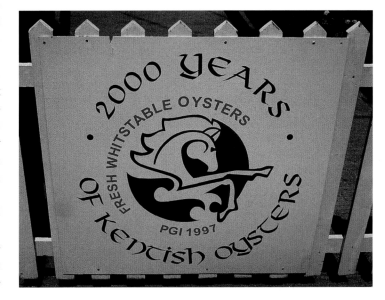

Quorn – a meat alternative – certainly appears to be a product for the future and has already made a significant inroad into the nation's shopping basket. First introduced in 1986, when it was presented in a pie, Quorn products contain myco-protein, a relative of the mushroom, with a high nutritional value.

Many first time consumers turn to Quorn for its dietary benefits – the products generally contain less fat and fewer calories than the meat alternatives, they contain little – in some cases no – cholesterol. And there are other 'plus points' – Quorn is always tender, absorbs seasoning well and can be cooked in many different ways – it's available in a growing number of products, including delicatessen lines, so can fit into differing lifestyles. That's an advantage that's been taken account of in the company's marketing strategies; Quorn is becoming well established as a brand in Europe, appearing in Switzerland as snichzels, saté in Holland etc. It's the product's versatility as well as its taste and texture that make it a success.

The company's own vision of the future is: As people increasingly heed the advice of health professionals and reduce the amount of fat and specifically saturated fat in their diets, meat free food will play an increasingly important role. This sea change in attitudes will grow, with health aware mums making a conscious choice to improve the family's diet – a long way from ethically driven vegetarianism which led the initial growth. Increasingly meat-less meals will become not only just acceptable but also desirable.

The choice of Quorn products is wide, with many 'heat to eat' offerings, but the following recipe, from Quorn, is an example of how it can be used as a cooking ingredient and the photo of the finished dish (opposite) shows how tempting it can be.

Right: Honey stall at the fair. Visited by Canadian beekeeper who asked how they dealt with the problem of bears – easy, the only bears in England are Teddy Bears!

Quorn Casserole

Heat the oil in a saucepan. Sauté the Quorn pieces and onion, cooking until the onion softens. Stir in the mushrooms, and sauté for further 3 minutes. Add the sweetcorn, stock, mustard and curry powder and bring to the boil, stirring continuously. Cover and simmer for 25 minutes.

Blend the cornflour into a paste with a little water. Stir into the mixture and continue stirring until the sauce thickens. Season to taste. Remove from the heat and stir in the Greek yoghurt. Serve with potatoes and seasonal vegetables.

2 tbs vegetable oil
350g Quorn pieces
1 large onion, chopped
200g mushrooms sliced
1/2 tsp chilli powder
400g tin sweetcorn
450ml vegetable stock
2 tbs wholegrain mustard
2 tsp curry powder
2 tbs cornflour
4 tbs Greek yoghurt
Salt and pepper

Opposite: Quorn Casserole

Above: A Hampshire Farmers' Market, just the place to buy Great British Food at its freshest and best, and, right, a detail from another in Bristol.

A millennium ago, producers – on however small a scale – took their wares to market, travelling a few miles to sell to customers who were also local.

Despite the vast changes of a thousand years, food is still produced by some, eaten by all. Produce must reach the consumer. Corner shops and supermarkets stock produce from all over this country and abroad and bring it within reach. Distribution, standardised quality control and many other factors, mean that most of the goods sold in these outlets come from large producers.

Right: This is the answer to the question: 'How many hen's eggs equals an ostrich egg'. Anyone for a really big helping of scrambled eggs?

The 're-invention' of **Farmers' Markets** brings the small, and sometimes very small, producer back in contact with the food buying public and the wheel has come full circle.

Apple growers bring fresh fruit and juice, to taste and to buy. Local cheesemakers offer their wares and will happily tell you how they made the soft goats cheese in the vine leaf wrapping, or about the cows fed on lush organic grass that provide the milk for the blue veined truckles. If it sounds like fun, then it is, and that's what it's intended to be. A lively, informative way for enthusiastic food

producers, however small, to bring their produce to market. Inevitably, as these are by definition local produce markets, there are no imported fruits or vegetables. It means the shopper has to cook seasonally, to focus on the excitement of the first of a crop: the early peas, sweet and tender enough to eat raw in salads, or the miniature early broad beans, delicious cooked in the pod, and the broad bean tops, cut early to save the grower from a later attack of blackfly and to provide an extra cash crop. Conversation is an important part of a farmer's market, growers like to share their culinary tips; farming can be a lonely life,

All recipes serve 4 unless otherwise stated

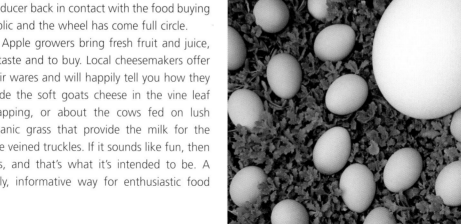

and these occasions provide contact with that most important person – the customer.

And talking about the wheel coming full circle, some supermarkets are encouraging local producers to set up stalls in their carparks on special 'market' days, bringing new customers to stallholders and 'something different' to supermarket regulars. Regional and county food associations are bringing their members' goods to the attention of food buyers for large and multiple stores and the catering industry.

The future taste of Britain – even better!
One of the surprising offerings at some farmer's markets is ostrich meat.

Right: A vision of the future in Britain?

Many **ostrich** farmers expect their produce to become a staple, rather than an exotic, food in the foreseeable future. Will the green fields of Britain so long grazed by placid cows and nibbled by woolly sheep become populated with tall, elegant, or, some say, absurd birds? It would make a delightful children's story, but the story might come true if the highly professional ostrich farmer has his way.

The following recipe is perfect for the busy cook, and an excellent way of trying ostrich meat for the first time.

Ostrich steaks

Marinade the steaks in the wine and half the oil seasoned with the bay leaf and a grind of black pepper, leave for two hours in a cool place. Drain and dry, heat the remaining oil and butter until lightly frothy, quickly fry the steaks for 2-3 minutes on each side – ostrich is best medium rare – put on heated serving dish, garnish with the watercress and serve with pasta dressed with oil and garlic.

700g ostrich steaks
275ml red wine
4 tbls olive oil
25g unsalted butter
Crumpled fresh bay leaf
Black pepper
Watercress

You only have to watch a few old Western movies to see that the **Hereford bull** was a prominent feature in producing quality beef in the 'good old days'. More than any other breed, the Hereford was responsible for producing the roast beef of 'olde England'. As a meat producer it's still to be found around

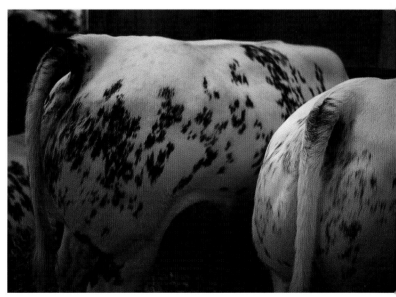

Below: The highly recognisable markings of the British Belgian Blue.

Britain today, but other breeds have, and are, still changing the livestock landscape of Britain. An example of this is the **British Short Horn**. It was exported to Belgium in the 1820s where it was developed as a dual purpose – beef and milk – animal. The beefing genetics of this breed – now called the Belgian Blue – were imported back into the UK in 1982, when research showed that it was comparable in growth and feed conversion to other beef breeds but with a much better meat to bone ratio. The British Belgian Blue is highly recognisable, with its blue patches on a cream background. From the Midlands northwards they have become a familiar sight. Their appeal to the farmer is in producing beef "which will meet 'supermarket' specifications and the hybrid vigour will increase performance at no extra cost... Some would say they are the breed for the Millennium." Quote from the Secretary, British Belgian Blue Cattle Society.

The development of new foods and food styles sometimes happens by fortunate coincidence. Take the fact that British international film star, Terence Stamp, is intolerant to gluten and that he has a friend who is in the food business. The combination led to 'The Stamp Collection' a superbly packaged organic range of products that includes British grown wheat-free flour and pastas.

If speed is a requisite for future food, then the following recipe from Pret à Manger, the highly successful sandwich bar group, is quick to prepare, quick to serve and full of fresh flavour and a perfect partner to a glass of chilled fruit juice.

Below: Cornflowers, glowing in the sun, attract helpful insects in biodiverse farming practices. They also attract the consumer to buy the equally flourishing vegetables.

Left: A logical way to get the organic message over - put it on the bag the food is sold in.

The Pret à Manger salmon roquette sandwich

Take the bread and cover first slice with the mayonnaise ensuring it's completely and evenly covered. Lay the poached salmon over the mayonnaise, once again taking care it is evenly distributed. Squirt 2 x 'Z's of lemon juice over the salmon. Season generously (salt and pepper mix). Evenly distribute the roquette over the sandwich

Their quote: 'it's nice and simple, very suited to the Millennium lifestyle as we all become more and more pushed for time!'

80g poached salmon
A handful of roquette
2 slices granary bread
A dollop of thick mayonnaise
2 squirts of lemon juice
A shiver of seasoning

Bio-dynamic farming sounds futuristic, but at its simplest it is self sustainability – a balanced crop-livestock system that provides produce in return for labour and does not rely on bought in foodstuffs and chemicals. It also involves creating a balance between crop growth and the energy provided by light, warmth and bio-dynamic preparations. It

All recipes serve 4 unless otherwise stated

Above: Immaculate polytunnels full of the 'cream of the crop'.

predators of crop pests. Poly tunnels are filled with bell peppers, aubergines and cucumbers, each with a glowing cluster of orange tagates – planted to encourage hoverflies, and other friendly 'bugs' to kill off greenfly and other unfriendly 'bugs'.

Everything tastes wonderful, but if you had to choose, perhaps the cheese is best of all. The only rind-washed cheddar-style cheese in the organic sector, made from the milk from the farm – the 2kg truckles mature for around nine months and are nutty, mellow and tangy all at once. It is sensational with the bread that – if you're lucky and they haven't sold out – you can also buy in the shop. Made by a local lady who learned her trade in Paris 30 years ago, and makes her own sourdough starter from grapes and kneads the bread by hand…

With the ever-growing interest in food, its quality and the different levels of enterprise that can be put to its production, bio-dynamic farming is inevitably set for a share of the spotlight. With its rigid controls it fits into the requirement for consumer awareness. At Old Plaw Hatch 350 families regularly buy an appreciable part of their food from this single 210 acre unit. It has proved that, as the method of farming is sustainable, with enough like minded participants, it is as a way of business.

seems like Utopia; if you are prepared to work hard, then it probably is.

The easy way to experience bio-diversity in action is to eat some of its results. Producers, processors and traders, if they pass rigorous inspections, and enter into binding contracts to conform with the rules of this type of farming, can be granted the right to use the "Demeter" and "Bio-dyn" trademarks.

Bio-dynamic farms generally encourage visitors. A perfect example is **Old Plaw Hatch** in West Sussex. Set in leafy countryside, there is an air of peaceful endeavour about the red brick farm buildings, a calm sense of the workers at one with the seasons. As with many bio-dynamic enterprises, this is based on a communal ownership, another reason for a sense of dedication. You can smell the quality of the produce on offer the moment you enter their farm shop – it's a basil scented summer. And it's busy in a leisurely way, there is always somebody buying milk – unpasturised and with a deep cream level from the Meuse-Rhine-Issel cows that placidly graze the thick green grass of 200 rolling acres. There are 9 acres of immaculate vegetables growing, dotted with clumps of cornflower and cosmos, with a small pond to entice friendly

Below: Imported to Britain, from Holland, by an American who makes cheese at Old Plaw Hatch Farm in West Sussex. Well worth his effort, because the result is a full flavoured, nutty cheddar type cheese, once tasted never forgotten.

Alma's Cheese Sauce

50g organic butter
2 medium sized onions
284ml Plaw Hatch single cream
650g Plaw Hatch Cheddar
20g fresh Plaw Hatch parsley
1 tsp wholegrain mustard
Seasoning

Melt the butter, chop the onions finely and braise in butter until golden brown. Stir in the cream, until quite hot. Melt the cheese in the cream. Stir for approximately 3-4 minutes to allow sauce to thicken. Add mustard and season to taste. Add finely chopped parsley. Sauce is very nice baked in the oven with macaroni with a sprinkling of Plaw Hatch cheese on top.

The above recipe was given by Jayne Thomas, one of the directors at Plaw Hatch; she had first enjoyed it a few evenings earlier when Alma, one of the visiting helpers from Europe, had cooked it for supper and served it with pasta. It was, she said, simply delicious, and an ideal way to enjoy the very special taste of Plaw Hatch cheese.

And how will eating out change? What, out of the dozens of new styles of cooking, will become so accepted that it is impossible to remember a time it wasn't always there? 'There is,' so the quote goes, 'nothing new under the sun.'

Be that as it may, the introduction of an Irish farmhouse-style restaurant in London in 1991 was certainly an innovation.

Its founder, Richard Willis, was of Irish descent and convinced that oysters and Guinness would take the capital by storm. In what could have been commercial suicide, there was no Scotch whisky to offer discerning diners – rather a selection of 15 Irish brands. It was hard to restrain their Irish chef's enthusiasm for fashionable Mediterranean dishes, but Colcannon – potatoes and scallions (Irish for onions) and champ – potatoes and cabbage, were soon satisfying a growing clientele. Helped by an interior design of Irish artefacts and pencil sketches of some

of her notable sons, Mulligan's of Mayfair won *Time Out*'s prestigious New Restaurant award.

It was the beginning of a great surge of Irish bars and today no town centre is without one, or often several, offering Irish-style hospitality. Mulligans, the one that started it all, is still there in the aptly named Cork Street, and the search continues for another trend setter.

Cooking with flowers fits perfectly into a future vision of leisure cooking. Imagine the calm oasis that a kitchen might become – no longer a hive of necessary activity, but an area for self expression.

The creative cook could take pleasure from arranging violets and pot marigolds, pansies and roses to delight the senses: sight, smell and even taste. Edible flowers are being grown in Britain and increasingly finding their way to market. If you like to grow your own then Courgette flowers appear in great profusion through the summer, a couple of plants in a tub or border can provide daily harvests. The following ideas are just a spring board for the imagination:

Below: Every one of these stunning dried flowers is, or rather was, edible. Perfect to hang up in the kitchen beside bunches of dried sage and mint.

All recipes serve 4 unless otherwise stated

Courgette flowers:

To prepare: pick or buy, wash gently, soak for few minutes in lightly salted water – to dislodge any lingering bugs – rinse and pat dry on kitchen paper

idea 1
Steam for 1-2 minutes, serve warm or cold with a dressing made of 1/3 lemon juice to 2/3 light olive oil. Serve with strips of char-grilled red pepper, slivers of anchovy and baby spring onions.

idea 2
Stuff flowers with pre-cooked brown and wild rice mixed with chopped fresh herbs, wedge the flowers upright in the steamer, tie their necks with a strand of fresh chive, steam for 1-2 minutes. Serve warm or chilled with a dressing of balsamic vinegar and hazelnut oil.

idea 3
Use the fresh flowers as an edible bowl for a small cluster of boiled quail eggs with snippets of roquette or nasturtium leaves. The eggs can either be in the shell for a hands-on lunch, or peeled and topped with a luscious home-made mayonnaise and sprinkled with marigold petals.

Other flowers are edible too: nasturtiums are good, as are edible pansies, violets, primroses and roses, but never eat anything that has been sprayed with chemicals.

Crystallised flowers:

Using a fine haired paintbrush, thinly cover the petals you wish to crystallise with a layer of egg white, then dust with caster sugar and dry in a warm place. These fragile shining delights should be used quickly; if you want to keep them for a while, then use gum arabic instead of egg white.

To decorate celebration cakes:

Primroses, for youth, are especially suitable for Christenings or Easter cakes. A sprinkling of violets for birthday cakes.

Crystallised flowers on ice cream, or mixed into a good vanilla ice cream, make a beautiful dessert – nasturtiums mixed into coffee ice is sensational.

Crystallised mint leaves with thick shards of grated chocolate sprinkled on a plain cheesecake, drizzled with cream flavoured with lavender sugar – a combination that bursts into flavour.

Fresh mint leaves painted with melted chocolate make the ultimate after dinner mint – best if made just before guests arrive. Use long stalks of mint, leaving the leaves on, and pass round in a tall glass so that you can 'pick you own'.

Paint rose petals with chocolate, tip with edible gold leaf, serve after dinner.

Opposite: The ingredients for 'idea 3', beautiful even before assembly.

A hundred years ago the Victorians spoke to each other with the blooms they gave, the following are just a few examples of their language of flowers: for culinary conversations a bouquet garni could hold hidden meaning, or a salad of flowers a message of friendship.

Angelica: inspiration
balm: sympathy
basil: Hatred, poverty
bay: glory, constancy
borage: Bluntness, energy
bramble: injustice, envy remorse
camomile: energy in adversity
corn: riches
cowslip: pensiveness, winning grace
crocus (saffron): mirth
dandelion: rustic oracle
elder: zealousness
fennel: merit
geranium (lemon): unexpected meeting
geranium (nutmeg): expected meeting
hop: injustice
lavender: diligence
marigold: anxiety
mint: virtue
nasturtium: patriotism
oats: the witching soul of music

pansy: thoughts
parsley: entertainment
peppermint: warmth of feeling
primrose: early youth
rose: love
deep red: bashful love
white, over two buds: secrecy
moss rose: ecstasy
moss rose bud: confession of love
rosemary: remembrance
sage: domestic virtue
thyme: activity
sweet violet: modesty

If cooking with flowers becomes part of the future art of entertaining, then eating them must become part of the art of living.

'The Art of Living' is the name of a series of Decorative Arts Fairs created and organised by the artist Elizabeth Organ, whose home and gallery is the Kilvert Gallery in Hay-on-Wye. The fairs combine interior design with fine art, local crafts with remarkable plants and, when they visit the South East of England, beautifully packaged regional speciality foods. Food with art, just one of the future tastes of Britain.

All recipes serve 4 unless otherwise stated

London

What would you like to eat?

Just about anything you can think of will be on offer somewhere in London.

Hundreds of varieties of 'foreign' cooking. All 'types' of cooking, vegetarian, vegan – and all kinds of ingredients. From the glorious, food-scented air of Harrods Food Hall, through the deliciously cool, inspirational shelves of Selfridges, to the narrow-fronted Aladdin's caves tucked away in London's 'villages' such as Chelsea and Battersea, there is food to cater for the diverse tastes and fancies of Londoners.

Take-aways and instant food are nothing new to London. In Dickens's day the pie shop provided the staple food of many Londoners; today there are the eel and pie shops, offering pies and 'liquor', or stewed eels fragrant with parsley, both with plenty of mashed potatoes to soak up the sauce. Earlier still were the bake houses where communal ovens provided cooking for a multitude with no form of cooking at home. Neither are 'exotics' new on the scene. Recent archaeologists' surprise at finding the remains of a banana in a sixteenth-century London rubbish tip inspired a flurry of letters to *The Times*; one came with a quote from Thomas Johnson who wrote a Herbal in 1597. Johnson's book included the

banana, and when revised in 1633 he mentions being given an unripe banana in April, that became ripe in May and lasted until June!

So what is Great British Food in London? There are classic venues, with classic menus. The Café Royal with food that tempted Oscar Wilde, the Ritz with teas that are synonymous with grand London. Going 'up West' – to the West End for a night out – has always meant a show and a meal, served in style, something to remember. The River Grill at the Savoy is a calm, unhurried oasis where excellent ingredients beautifully cooked have delighted visitors for 200 years.

Opposite: Harrods… could be called a national institution.

Below: A polished bar and shining bottles, a welcoming pub, haven in the bustling city.

Above: Fortnums, essential London.

Away from the splendid architecture of The Strand are the discrete delights of Liberty's coffee shop and Fortnum and Mason's famous Fountain, where a wander on through the store itself leads to elegantly arranged edible temptations.

Covent Garden, some few hundred yards from the Savoy, is bustling, colourful and exciting – a tourist's delight. It used to be just as busy at 4 in the morning when it was the Capital's fruit and vegetable market. Now that activity has gone to the more industrially accessible South Bank of the Thames. Trade has a cookable history in London – the Smithfield meat market… Spittlefields…

Fashion and food have always been closely linked – the seriously garlicky **Bloomsbury soup** was a favourite of the Bloomsbury 'set': Virginia Woolf, Vanessa Bell and friends. Like them, it was a touch outrageous, the taste and smell enough to take one's breath away, like them its appearance initially deceptive, coolly subtle.

Food to look out for in London is essentially the trend of the day. Sushi developed its popularity in specialist restaurants, now it's in supermarkets. **Organic produce** was once only found in wholefood shops, now it's widespread, destined to become standard fare.

London has always been the recipient of Britain's 'bounty'. The Old Kent Road, through the memorably named Elephant and Castle, used to be a drovers' route, where flocks of sheep, fattened on the lush pastures of Kent, walked their way to the tables of town.

Below: Biltong as made in London - meat dried in strips - as you can read in many Edwardian ' boys' adventures' is the perfect stuff to have in your pocket on safari. It's also very good as part of as assorted hors d'oeuvre, or sliced into a casserole. Some enterprising producers are even making tuna biltong, delicious sliced paper thin with a squeeze of lemon juice.

Fishmonger's fare

A perfect recipe to enjoy the fine quality of fresh, and smoked, fish on offer in London.

Fish and Smoked Salmon Terrine

Chill all ingredients thoroughly. Line an ovenproof dish with silicone paper – 9x22 cm base for a classic terrine, or a 1lb loaf tin. Separate two of the eggs, reserving the yolks for a later mayonnaise. Put the egg whites, the whole egg, chopped cod, grated rind of the lemon and 1 tablespoon of the juice, a quick shake of tabasco in a chilled blender and process until smooth. Put mixture in the refrigerator for 15 minutes. Add cream to mixture, process again until smooth. Pour half the mixture into the terrine, cover with sliced smoked salmon, top with remaining mixture, cover with cooking foil, then place in an oven dish with enough water in to come two-thirds of the way up the cooking dish. Put in a moderate oven for an hour, cool quickly then refrigerate for 2 hours. Slice to serve. It looks its best without any adornment, wedges of lemon offered separately. Serve with Melba toast.

500g skinned cod fillet
3 eggs
1 lemon
600ml cream
125g smoked salmon
Tabasco sauce

Harrods **Food Halls** could be called a national institution. When tea merchant, Charles Henry Harrod, opened a corner shop in Knightsbridge a century and a half ago the area was a haunt of 'vagabonds and ladies of the night'. Today it's a prime London location and a magnet for Londoners and visitors alike.

Almost all the meat sold in the Meat Hall is British – including lamb from the owner's, Mohamed Al Fayed's, Scottish estate. Harrods Stilton comes from Webster's Dairy, Saxelbye,

Above: Old Father Thames - the river that brought prosperity to London also brought the tradition of eating Whitebait. Wash and dry the tiny silvery fish, shake them in a bag contain a spoonful of flour well seasoned with cayenne pepper. Dust off loose flour, fry quickly in hot oil until crisp, turn onto draining paper, season with salt and pepper. Eat instantly.

one of the smallest dairies in the country. It is matured for 16 weeks to give it a specially rich creaminess. Rhodda of Redruth in Cornwall churns the clotted cream butter on offer -'the richest butter you could taste, if you want real indulgence, this is it.' There are 250 types of bread in the Bakery Department, most of which are baked in-house. There's even a Harrod's Ale and there are 140 chefs working in 20 professional kitchens to provide fresh goods for the Food Halls. All in all, it's a place of superlatives and a show case for much of the Best of British.

Flour Power City supplies restaurants all over London with delicious breads such as Organic baguettes, Sourdough made with roasted potato and Rye levian. Mathew Jones, ex Mezzo chef, is a bakery enthusiast who uses mainly organic ingredients, and a hands on knowledge gained from working in a string of top flight restaurants. You can buy direct from their bakery in Shoreditch, and at the bustling Borough Market.

Having bought the bread, how about some pâté? Coquus – Traiteur Artisanal, also to be found at Borough Market, make pâtés and terrines in the 'good old fashioned way', with the freshest ingredients and tender loving care. Some rabbit terrine with rosemary and olives would be perfect alongside a selection of cheeses from Neal's Yard Dairy who venture out from Covent Garden to bring British cheeses to the same marketplace

For the following recipe, use one of the many specialist butchers in individual shops or the food halls of London to buy tiny, tender quail and ask them to spatchcock the birds for you.

Choosing the wine to cook with can be a regional adventure – white, red or rosé – all are produced in Britain by vineyards large and small. White wine might seem the obvious choice to use in this recipe, but red makes a dish with gusto, and rosé an almost perfumed offering – the choice is yours.

All recipes serve 4 unless otherwise stated

Quail with risotto

If your supplier hasn't spatchcocked the quails, then do-it-yourself by splitting them down the backbone with kitchen scissors, pressing them flat, and making them stay that way by putting a skewer through – first one wing, then through the breast bone, then the other wing. Rub half the fresh herbs into the skin of the quails, paint them with a little olive oil and set them aside while you start the risotto.

Melt the butter with 2 tablespoons of the olive oil in a frying pan, add the onion, sliced, and the garlic, crushed. Cook gently until all is tender, then add the washed, rinsed and dried rice and stir well over heat for a few minutes. Add the wine, meanwhile heat the stock. Heat a dribble of olive oil in another frying pan, lay the quail in, skin side down, pressing them down, cook for 2-3 minutes over a medium heat until brown, turn over and do the same again, put in a medium oven for 5 minutes to cook through.

When the wine has been absorbed by the rice, add the stock, stir, and keep stirring the rice from time to time as you cook the quail. Take the quail out of the oven and put on a hot serving dish. In a few minutes the rice should be cooked – creamy and delicious – take off the heat, stir in the grated cheese, sprinkle over the herbs and serve with the quail.

4 fresh spatchcocked quail
250ml regional wine
450ml chicken or vegetable stock
1 medium red onion
2 cloves of garlic
3 tbs olive oil
2 tbs butter
250g arborio rice
30g grated hard cheese (regional)
2 tbs fresh chopped herbs

Below: Called 'The Garden Roast', the name of this dish, made of roast vegetables from all over the world, comes from Covent Garden Market, where the chef bought his ingredients.

Indian restaurants feature in almost every town in Britain, and London has its share of them, large and small. Curry is one of the nation's favourite meals, and a quick glance along most supermarket chill counters offers a continually growing choice: Chicken Korma, Chicken Tikka Masala, Lamb Roganjosh or Thai Green or Red Curries and delicious rice dishes: Moghlai Pilau, Masala Pilau are only some of the tempting offerings.

Above: A deliciously spicy dish from Noon's - one of the reasons why Britain's favourite dish is curry.

Many of these dishes are made by **Noon Products**, based at Southall. This is a company at the forefront of quality food production and their Chairman, G.K. Noon, M.B.E, has his own recipe for their success: "Pick a team of skilled buyers to source the finest herbs and ingredients available in the world; add a large helping of experienced chefs, combine them in the right proportions; process the lot in the blender of a sophisticated plant buzzing with the latest technology; add a dash of personal love and care and – voila! You have Noon Products."

They make over a million chilled and frozen ready-made Indian meals a month and you can find them in British outlets such as Waitrose, Harrods and Sainsburys. The professionalism of their food is obvious from the scale of their production, their commitment to taste – the use of the finest herbs and spices, a battery of talented chefs and recipes that work such as the following "Indian Feast", given by Noon Products.

All recipes serve 4 unless otherwise stated

An Indian Feast

Chicken Tikka Makhani

Mix all powder and paste ingredients together with oil and yoghurt. Add chicken pieces and mix well, coating all chicken pieces. Leave marinated chicken for at lest two hours. Cook under hot grill until done.

Liquidise tomatoes. Heat oil, add finely chopped onions, cook until light brown. Add ginger, garlic and green chilli paste one at a time cooking each for a few minutes. Add all powder spices and salt one at a time starting with red chilli powder and cooking each for a few minutes. Add liquidised tomatoes and cook until oil starts to separate. Add single cream gradually, mixing continuously. Add chicken tikka pieces and fresh coriander. Bring to boil. Serve hot with paratha or rice.

Opposite: Vegetable Jalfrezi

Chicken Tikka:
500g boneless chicken breast – cut into 1" cubes
70g natural yoghurt
1 tsp fresh garlic paste
1 tsp fresh ginger paste
1/2 tsp fresh green chillies paste
1/2 tbs garam masala powder
1/4 tsp fenugreek
1 tbsp paprika
1/2 tsp red chilli powder
Salt to taste
4 tbs vegetable oil
Serves 4-6

Makhani sauce
10 tbs vegetable oil
1 tsp fresh garlic paste
150g chopped onions
1 tsp fresh ginger paste
1/2 tsp green chillies paste
1 tsp red chilli powder
3 tbs paprika
1.5 tbs garam masala powder
1/2 tsp fenugreek powder
Salt to taste
15g chopped fresh coriander
700g tomatoes tinned
250ml single cream

Masala dal

7 tbs vegetable oil
1 tsp cumin seeds
1 tsp fresh garlic paste
60g sliced onions
1 tsp fresh ginger paste
1/2 tsp fresh green
chillies paste
1/2 tsp red chilli powder
1/2 tsp turmeric
1 tsp coriander powder
1 tsp cumin powder
1/2 tsp garam masala
10g fresh coriander
225g chopped tinned
tomatoes
Salt to taste
800g cooked channa dal
(yellow lentils)
Lemon juice
1/2 lemon
Serves 4-6

Cook channa dal with salt, turmeric and water until fully cooked. Heat oil, add cumin seeds and crackel. Add sliced onions and cook until light brown. Add garlic, ginger and green chilli paste one at a time, cooking each for a few minutes.

Add all dry powder spices and salt one at a time, cooking each for a few minutes and sprinkle half the quantity of fresh coriander. Add chopped tomatoes, cook until the oil starts to separate. Add the cooked channa dal, mix well and bring to boil.

Lastly add lemon juice and the other half of the fresh coriander. Serve hot with rice.

Lemon Pillau

Heat oil until frying hot, add mustard seeds and cumin seeds – crackle. Add Channa Dal, Urid Dal and cashew nuts cook until cashew nuts are lightly browned. Add curry leaves, rice, salt and turmeric, sauté until turmeric has mixed thoroughly. Add hot water 2.5 times by volume of rice along with the juice from the lemons. Bring to boil mixing occasionally. Boil until all water is visibly absorbed. Cover rice with greaseproof paper and lid the container. Reduce heat, steam until cooked. Remove and serve.

7tbs vegetable oil
1tsp mustard seeds
10g urid dal (white
lentils)
10g channa dal (yellow
lentils)
1 tsp cumin seeds
20g cashew nuts
A few curry leaves
400g Basmati rice
1 tsp turmeric
Salt to taste
Water by volume
Fresh lemon – cut into
quarters
2 lemons

Right: One of the famous London pubs - The Grenadier in Wilton Row.

Vegetable Jalfrezi

50ml vegetable oil
1 tbs cumin seeds
200g sliced onions
2 tsp fresh garlic paste
2 tsp fresh ginger paste
1 tsp fresh green chillies paste
1 tsp red chilli powder
1 tsp turmeric
2 tbs coriander powder
2 tbs cumin powder
1.5 tsp garam Masala
1.5 tsp fenugreek
Salt to taste
15g fresh coriander
65g tomato purée
200g chopped tinned tomatoes
40g fresh green peppers
40g fresh red peppers
100g baby corn
100g batton carrots
100g beans
100g cauliflower
Water if required
Serves 4-6

Boil water, add salt, blanch carrots, beans, cauliflower, baby corn – drain and keep aside. Heat oil, add cumin seeds and crackle, add sliced onions and cook until clear. Add garlic, ginger, green chilli paste cooking each for a few minutes. Add all the powder spices one at a time, cooking each for a few minutes. Add half of the fresh coriander and cook until oil starts to separate.

Add tomato purée and stir for a few minutes. Add chopped tomatoes and dilute with water if required. Bring to boil and simmer until the oil starts to separate. Add red and green peppers, cook until half done. Add rest of all the vegetables. Mix and simmer, sprinkle with the rest of the corainder and mix. Serve hot.

Paratha

Mix wholemeal flour (Atta) and salt, make a well in the middle, add warmed oil and hot water just sufficient to coax the mix into a pliable dough. Rest it for at least 30 minutes, covered with a moist cloth or in a plastic bag. Put the dough back on board and knead thoroughly until it does not stick to the palms. Divide into lemon shaped balls. Roll into a circle dusting each ball with flour if necessary. Coat with warm oil using a brush, cut an incision from the middle of the circle to the edge and roll into a cone. Press the cone from the edge to the point – roll the flattened circles into pancake shapes and cook over a hot thick bottomed frying pan or griddle on both sides until done. Brush each side with oil and serve

500g wholemeal flour
200g warm water
200g warm oil
8g salt
Serves 4-6

After such a magnificent feast, a cool English dessert of **strawberries** would be perfect; serve simply with cream and sugar, or for a change try one of the following recipes for the scarlet fruits of summer.

The last Monday in the month of July is the time for 'Swan-Upping' on the River Thames when the Vintners and Dyers Companies have the right to claim a quantity of cygnets between Henley and London Bridge.

In Elizabeth 1st's day swan was considered a feast – now it's more likely to be considered a pet! But Henley is linked with edible delights when its world famous regatta is taking place and strawberries are in season.

Left: The skyline of London is very much a mix of ancient and modern. This particular skyscraper is of the temporary kind, being made of sandwiches, the staple lunch of many of the commuters to the capital.

All recipes serve 4 unless otherwise stated

Strawberry water ice

(for serious heatwaves)
Wash, dry the strawberries and sieve or
liquidise them, meanwhile dissolve the
sugar in the water, bring to the boil, boil
for 5 minutes. Squeeze the citrus fruit.
When the syrup is cold, mix everything
together, pour into a shallow tray and
freeze. Before serving put into the 'fridge
for 30 minutes.

450g hulled strawberries
110g granulated sugar
1 tbs citrus juice (lemon,
orange or mixture)
4 tbs water

Eton mess

*The tradition that this delicious strawberry
dish came from Eton College may or may
not be true, but the result is arguably one
of the most delicious ways to serve this
essential Summer fruit.*

First, mash the strawberries, preferably
with a silver fork and in a pretty bowl!
Add the strawberries to the thick cream
that's ready in another pretty bowl, stir
in gently, taste and add sugar if you
have to. Eat in a warm, sunny garden.

110g fresh strawberries
50g thick farm fresh
dairy cream
Sugar to taste

*Left: Perfect summer fruits
make a perfect dinner
table centrepiece that can
be consumed at leisure
with the coffee.*

Places to eat

Asking a Londoner to recommend some modern British restaurant is rather like asking someone who works in Thorntons famous chocolate factory to tell you their favourite confections - both of which are spoilt for choice. Trying the exercise on regular 'eaters out' yeilded a rich harvest - The Ivy Restaurant, West Street 0207 8364751, Bluebird in The Kings Road 0207 559 1000 and Vth Floor in Sloane Street, 0207 235 5250.

Asking the managing director of a famous eatery to describe it will inevitably result in a glowing recommendation, the following quote from Joseph Levine could be luminous but it would still be true.

"The Greenhouse Restaurant in Hay's Mews by Berkeley Square is as popular today as it was twenty-five years ago. Tucked away behind its private garden in a peaceful Mayfair mews, the atmosphere is English Country House, with the emphasis on peace, relaxation and the very best of British ingredients in the kitchen."

Alastair Little believes in 'cooking with conscience'. His hugely successful restaurant at 49 Frith Street, Soho, in the heart of eating-out London, is a testament to his belief. It features short, frequently changing menus combining the finest seasonal produce with dishes designed with sensitivity and flair. 'Alastair Little' opened 15 years ago at the forefront of the creation of modern British food. 'Alastair Little Lancashire Road', London W2, runs on the same principles - including making their own pickles and chutneys on site. It has a stronger emphasis on Italian cooking - because he likes it - and is a little cheaper - 'because it's not Soho".

Cheeseboard

Buy a complete selection at Paxton and Whitfield, Jermyn Street, 0171 930 0259 cheesemongers since 1797.

Left: Billingsgate, the great fish market that serves London and the home counties, providing top quality and freshness for the rapidly growing number of speciality fish restaraunts.

All recipes serve 4 unless otherwise stated

kent

Over two-thirds of Kent is bordered by the sea so it's not surprising that fish features strongly on pub menus around the county. Fresh, locally caught cod, or rock salmon – called huss at the coast – served deep fried in a crispy beer batter is the perfect partner for chips made from Thanet's deservedly famous potatoes.

From Folkestone, on the south coast, the **Fisherman's Co-operative** services the retail and catering trade nationally, the majority of their range being caught by their own fleet of trawlers. They also sell direct to the public from The Stade on the edge of the picturesque harbour. Their undyed smoked haddock is delicious lightly poached and served with a knob of fresh butter.

A drive around the coast to Dungeness leads to a vast, shingle bird sanctuary dotted with low-lying cottages including the unusual homes of several artists and sculptors. Hand painted signs lead across the shingle to a fisherman who smokes and sells his varied catch, including, at times, the green fleshed garfish, a miniature swordfish look-a-like.

On the north coast, **Seasalter Shellfish**, on the quay beside the working harbour at Whitstable, has origins prior to the Magna Carta. Today it is the main supplier of oyster seed in the UK and dispatches to oyster growers all over Europe. It also sells ready-to-eat oysters by the dozen at Whitstable and by mail order. Thoughtfully, they also sell oyster knives. A dozen or so plump oysters and a bottle of the crisply delicious Biddenden Vineyard Cider – made with local apples and skill – enjoyed in a sheltered corner of a sunny beach make for a memorable taste of Kent. If you don't like the idea of consuming oysters raw then try them rolled in smoked salmon and lightly grilled or tuck a few into a beefsteak before frying it and call the sensational result a 'carpetbag'.

Opposite: Autumn harvest: Hops to flavour beer or to string over a country mantelpiece.

Left: Whitstable harbour has a fascinating mixture of commercial and leisure boats as well as an excellent café - specialising in local caught fish. These sheds are used to store nets, and others are used as a place to cook whelks.

The following recipe, and 'legend', was given by Seasalter Shellfish (Whitstable) Limited:

Cioppino

24 fresh Whitstable oysters

450g white fish

1/2 kilo fresh small clams

450g cockles

2 tbs olive oil

2 tbs butter

3 large onions, chopped

4 cloves garlic, minced

1 green pepper, chopped

1 can Italian plum tomatoes

2 cups light fish stock

2 glasses dry white wine

Tomato purée

Oregano, basil, cayenne pepper and marjoram

According to the San Francisco legend, the fishermen along the wharf used to keep pots of boiling water flavoured with tomatoes, garlic and onion into which any unsold fish would be thrown. The fishermen would cry 'Chip-in, chip-in' as they asked for more fish for the stew and, as many of them were from Southern Italy, an 'O' was added. Thus 'Cioppino' was created. Whatever the truth behind the name, Cioppino has now developed into a delicate balance of seafood, wine and tomatoes, but there is really no accurate recipe as every day it would be different, depending on the day's catch.

Fresh oysters, clams, cockles and white fish are all readily available in Whitstable so we have based our Cioppino on these ingredients. However, prawns, mussels and crab can also be used – in fact practically any fish or shellfish you can think of!

Heat the butter in a large pot, add the onions and garlic, cook stirring gently until onions are light brown, then add peppers and cook until they soften. Add tomatoes, tomato purée, herbs and fish stock, then allow to simmer for 30 minutes. Add wine, salt and pepper to taste and continue simmering. Add clams, cover and cook for two minutes. Add cockles and white fish, cover again and cook for further thirty minutes. Finally add the oysters with their liquor and cook for one minute. Serve in warm bowls with crusty garlic bread.

One of the best ways to get a feel of an area is on foot. Leaving the car behind means you can hear the birds sing, smell the wildflowers and – important in an area as famed for its hop growing as Kent – have a beer with lunch or supper. The first South East Walking Festival, in September 1999, was based at Wye, the setting for one of Britain's oldest universities. It is a tranquil village – except during the University's rag week. Walkers have passed this way since Chaucer's time on their pilgrimage to Canterbury. Even the local brew has an ancient history. **Shepherd Neame**, brewing at Faversham, is one of Britain's oldest brewers and can trace its beginnings back to 1698. Try their 'Bishop's Finger' – Kentish Strong Ale – or their bottle-conditioned 'Spitfire'. The Sun inn at Faversham is owned by the company. It is oak beamed and welcoming, everything a traditional pub should be, but its menu changes with food fashion – you can sometimes enjoy a tempting dish shown in a Sunday newspaper colour supplement on the following Monday lunchtime – fast food indeed!

Opposite: Cioppino.

left: Easily accessible from London, the Garden of England, as Kent has been known from the 15th century, has long attracted the famous in search of good food and drink - as shown by visitors to the Crown Inn at Sarre.

All recipes serve 4 unless otherwise stated

Soft fruit ices, sorbets, ice creams, or frozen desserts.

Frozen soft fruit prepared – destriggred currants, topped-and-tailed gooseberries – before freezing.

Dairy cream, or crème fraiche, or fromage frais, or yoghurt – thick or thin, or non milk creams, or coconut milk or cream, etc.

Sugar or honey to taste

Alcohol – a dash of something delicious, Drambuie to go with raspberries, Pernod with blackcurrants, or champagne with white currants for example. Or a non alcoholic cordial, perhaps ginger, or elderflower.

This is more of a method than a recipe. It's ideal for using fruit that you bought at a 'pick your own' venue or grew, or simply bought in bulk and stored in the freezer. Try it once, and you'll be converted to the no-nonsense method that lets you improvise for ever, and never be lost for an instant, stunning dessert.

Spoon frozen fruit into the blender, a wine glassful per serving. Most blenders work best about half full, so it may have to be done in batches.

Whiz for long enough to break frozen fruit down into granular 'mush'. Tip in half as much cream (or whatever you're using) as fruit, one more brief whiz, taste, add sweetener of honey or whatever to taste, final whiz, pile into chilled serving glasses, pour over – if you like – a dash of extra flavour, an alcohol or squeeze of lime. The perfect – very nearly instant – frozen dessert.

Garden of England apples and ginger

1 large Cox's Orange Pippin
13mm piece of fresh ginger
Tsp butter
Heaped tsp organic sugar

A quick, but sensational pudding. Serve with ice cold untreated cream for maximum impact.

Peel and then slice the ginger as thinly as possible. Melt the butter in a frying pan, add the ginger slices and cook gently until the ginger is transparent, add the thickly sliced and cored – but not peeled – apples, turn up the heat and fry quite fiercely until the outside of the apples are beginning to brown, turn the heat down, add the sugar, cook briefly whilst stirring gently until the sugar has melted, serve at once.

In Cockney rhyming slang 'apples and pears' means 'stairs'. Both fruits are very much garden of England produce and widely grown in the county.

February 14th is St Valentine's Day. If heart-shaped chocolates aren't to your liking – or even if they are – why not try pears poached in elderberry wine and scented with rosewater as a romantic dessert?

Pears in the Pink

Elderberry wine has such a deep, fruity flavour that in Victorian times it was sometimes sold as a counterfeit Burgundy.

Half bottle of elderberry wine
4 well shaped pears
175g organic sugar
Tbs rosewater
8 cloves
Dessertspoon arrowroot

Choose pears with nice round 'bottoms' and slender 'necks', peel them and halve lengthways, remove the stalk and core. Place the pears and wine in a deep saucepan, bring to simmering point and cook gently until just tender – about 15 mins. When ready remove the pears with a slotted spoon and lay them on a serving dish, 'bottoms up' to make heart shapes. Dissolve the sugar in the wine then stir in the arrowroot that has been mixed with a little water to a smooth paste, bring back to the boil briefly until it thickens, take off the heat and stir in the rosewater. Using a clove as a decorative 'nail' put one in each pear half at the opposite end to the stalk. Pour the wine over the pears and serve with whipped cream ...and a kiss!.

Opposite: Perfect pears make a delicious starter filled with stilton, wrapped in air dried ham and dressed with port.

All recipes serve 4 unless otherwise stated

There is a vast choice of apple juices available today, many are single varietal, such as Cox or Bramley, and it's fascinating to taste the difference. A visit to **Brogdale Horticultural Trust** in Faversham will show you just how many types of apple there are – they have over 4000 varieties of apples, plums, pears, cherries, quince, medlar, peach, apricot and cobnut. When you've found a favourite, or concocted your own blend, it's fun to try it as a refreshing sorbet that could even be served in a scooped out apple 'shell'.

Below: Varietal apple juice from Brogate – simply delicious!

the pan off the heat, tip it to one side and carefully light the alcoholic haze with a taper. Be careful! Keep your hands well away, and don't be tempted to lean over and breathe in the delicious smell. When all is calm, mix the two liquids, let them get quite cold and then put into an ice cream maker or freeze in a shallow tin, beat two or three times during freezing. Keep frozen until you want to enjoy the Sorbet, then put in the fridge for 30mins before serving.

Wild duck with sloe and orange sauce

Wild ducks can be found in specialist butchers, or at times direct from a shoot – a cottage on the main road from Goudhurst to Cranbrook has a sign up in the winter if any are available. The wild fowl taste very different from farmyard ones – they have darker flesh and a distinctive, gamey flavour. They are also quite small and are often served as half a duck per portion – even then they may need stretching by the addition of stuffing balls or small, spicey sausages.

1 brace of wild duck
110g butter
4 juniper berries
3 tbs sloe jelly – or other tart fruit jelly
Salt and pepper
Tsp arrowroot

Wipe and then dry the birds inside and out, crush the juniper berries, mix them into the butter and stuff this inside the ducks. Put in an oven dish, cover with foil, put into an oven heated to gas mark 6/400F/200C, after 15 minutes turn the heat down to 4/350F/180C and cook for 40-50 minutes in all, until tender. Baste occasionally with the juices in the dish. Take the birds from the oven, put them on a hot serving dish, then leave in a warm place while you make the sauce. Tip any excess fat off the juices in the pan, add the squeezed juice of the orange and the sloe jelly, boil up quickly, add salt and pepper to taste then thicken with the arrowroot dissolved in a little

The handsome cardoon grows easily, is generally winter hardy, and the immature flower heads can be cooked, and served, like globe artichokes. They make an unusual accompaniment to game dishes.

Serious Sorbet

For perfection the apple brandy should be that made in Somerset – if you can't find it then Calvados or even straightforward brandy is still very good. Put the apple juice, glucose, icing sugar and juice of the lemon in a saucepan, stirring to dissolve the sugar. Bring it just to the boil then remove from heat. Now comes the exciting part, the apple brandy has to be flamed to burn off the alcohol or it won't freeze. In a small pan heat the apple brandy slowly until you can see fumes coming up from the surface, take

500ml unsweetened apple juice
100g icing sugar
70g liquid glucose
1 lemon
25ml apple brandy

All recipes serve 4 unless otherwise stated

water, boil to thicken and serve with the duck. Buttered noodles, or perhaps a mixture of mashed potatoes and celeriac go very well with this, followed by a refreshing orange and fresh mint salad.

Another seasonal pleasure that is sometimes sold 'at the farmgate' is the **broad bean**. The grey green leaves and purple flowers of broad beans make them handsome enough to grow in the flower border and, as an added incentive to putting them in a decorative setting, their perfume on a sunny day is intense.

Young broad beans can be boiled in their pods and served, and eaten complete, with melted butter and a sprinkling of fresh herbs. As they get older the beans need taking out of their velvet lined pods, and finally at the end of the season it's even worth removing the hard outer shell of each bean before boiling. They seem to have a natural affinity with parsley sauce and are excellent served with boiled ham and mashed potatoes. Early in the season you sometimes see broad bean tops – that is the leafy tops of the plants – for sale. They are very good steamed. Cutting the tops provides an early cash crop for the grower and also means that blackfly don't get such a grip on the plants later so it's a double bonus and reduces the need for pesticides.

In Victorian times 7000 acres of **cobnuts** were grown in Britain; now it's around 250 acres. Enterprising growers in Kent are raising consumer awareness of these delicious nuts by selling them covered in chocolate, and producing recipe booklets for them. With luck the rural delights of cobnut orchards – locally known as 'plats' – will reappear and the following recipe become a standard rather than an unusual treat.

Far right: The grapes aren't ready yet in this Kentish vineyard but if the leaves haven't been sprayed, they can be blanched and rolled around savoury rice and baked until tender in vegetable stock, or used to line a casserole of quail or chicken pieces bathed in white wine and herbs.

All recipes serve 4 unless otherwise stated

Cobnut Brownies

Cobnuts are so beautiful with their soft brown elegant shells nestling in 'pixie cap' leafy cups that it almost seems a shame to crack them. These Brownies can be made with hazelnuts, but if you can find cobnuts they are just a little more special.

Dry fry the nuts, or toast them under the grill for a few minutes until their skin becomes papery and you can rub it off, chop the nuts into large pieces. Melt the chocolate and butter together and then stir in the sugar. Beat the eggs to a froth, add the chocolate mixture, beat again, sieve in the flour and cocoa powder, folding it into the mixture and finally add the nuts. Spread the mixture into a lined 10x12" (25.5 x 30cm) baking tray (use silicon paper). Bake for 20mins at gas mark 4/350F/180C, they should still be a bit soft, leave to cool, then cut into squares, dust with icing sugar and enjoy.

50g shelled cobnuts
110g butter
110g dark chocolate
235g dark sugar
225g self raising flour
25g cocoa powder
1 dessertspoon icing sugar
4 large free range eggs

The Merchant Farmer's Kentish Hop Biscuits

110g stoneground wholemeal flour

110g medium oatmeal

50g soft brown sugar

Good pinch ground sea salt

1/2 tsp bicarbonate of soda

1tsp dried ground hops

75g English butter

1 small free range egg

Oven temp:
gas mark 5/375F/190C

Hop biscuits are delicious with soft curd cheese, such as Syndale Valley Cheesemakers' flavoured with garlic. The rich, nutty taste of oatmeal is given a unique tang by the dried hops, in late summer you could use a sprinkling of fresh hop petals, perhaps even gathering them from the hedgerows. For another taste, leave out the hops, and add a teaspoonful of the Merchant Farmer's grainy mustard – found at real food shops all over Kent.

Mix together all the dry ingredients, rub in the butter. Beat the egg separately and add enough of it to the mixture to make a stiff dough. Turn out onto a surface sprinkled with flour and oatmeal and roll 1/5" (4mm) deep for thin biscuits, 1/2" (13mm) for 'flat breads'. Cut to required shapes, 3" (7.5mm) circles, oblongs etc. Bake for 10-15 minutes, until just turning golden. Cool on a wire rack. When cold store in an airtight container.

Above: A colourful display of regional products on the 'Kentish Fare' barrow, much of it made from fruit and vegetables grown in the county.

Right: Early Spring, and you can still see agile hop stringers on stilts in some hop gardens although a growing number are using mechanical lifts.

Opposite: Grapes on the vine, too sharp to eat, but perfect for wine.

Food interest events

Rochester Dickensian Christmas Street Fair with on-street Chinese cooking, Whitstable Oyster Festival and Regatta, Mount Ephraim Summer Fruit festival, Kent Show, Brogdale Cider and Perry Festival

Cheeseboard

Luddesdown with Tarragon and Shallots - a fresh goat's cheese from Rochester. *Basing smoked goat's cheese* – from Edenbridge. *A large Coulommier with peppercorns* from Syndal Valley Cheesemakers in Sittingbourne.

All recipes serve 4 unless otherwise stated

south

Surrey • East Sussex • West Sussex

east

In the 1960s visitors to the South of England looked forward to finding a pub that stocked Merrydown's **country wines**. A glass of elderberry or sloe, or a schooner of the infamously strong cider, was as much a part of long summer evenings as the open topped sports car and the Brigitte Bardot headscarf. Today, the Merrydown fruit wines have a new name – Both Barrels, but they're still a real country taste when you find them at their home base in Horam, East Sussex.

The regional brewers, Harvey & Son in Lewes, county town of East Sussex, have been producing fine beers since 1790. And they must be good because their loyal band of followers have even been known to threaten to boycott a pub that was considering changing to a national brew.

If you're feeling like a physical as well as a gastronomic challenge, then it would be worth visiting the Lurgashall Winery in Petworth, West Sussex. Alongside their own traditional country wines they'll offer you mead and liqueurs and you might like to consider your choice while admiring their 17th-century barn, or Elizabethan herb garden. If you would like to take a little longer you could enjoy their orienteering course!

Another Sussex 'brew' is Gran Steads Ginger Wine – no alcohol but a delicious 'kick'

Opposite: A fashion show of pumpkins and squashes. Lots of different ways to cook lots of varieties but all can be oven roasted in a little oil and finished with toasted pumpkin seeds for extra bite.

and their stand, complete with tasting, is always a great success at agricultural shows. The English wine renaissance achieved a memorable success at the 1999 Vinexpo held in France when the Carr Taylor Vineyard won the best sparkling wine category. This was in a blind tasting and against 4,000 other wines from France and Italy.

Many farm shops and country outlets stock Gordon's **Mustards**, with over 30 different specialities, they take mustard into new realms.

Another widely found brand in the south is **Loseley**. All their yoghurts, creams and cottage cheese are made with milk from the Loseley Jersey herd that you can often see grazing the pasture around Losely Park near Guildford. Driving on to Plaistow, nr Billingshust, you can enjoy the milk of the other great Channel Island dairy breed at **Rumbolds Farm Dairy**, where their Guernsey herd supplies the milk, cheese and butter that they sell from the farm.

Above: Dexter parade at a South East agricultural show: The livestock ring at the agricultural show is the place to see farm animals in the peak of condition taking their owners for a walk!.

Below: Just some of the dairy product made from the Loseley Jersey herd.

Farm-made **cheeses** are very much a taste of the south. Mark and Sarah Hardy, at Sussex High Weald Dairy, use sheep's and organic cows' milk to make a wide range of products, all suitable for vegetarians. Their Ashdown Foresters was a winner at the Organic Farm awards, and just right to enjoy as part of a picnic on the Ashdown Forest. The Ashdown Forest, in East Sussex, is Winnie the Poo country. It's no longer a 'forest' in the true sense, but a beautiful heather-covered heath punctuated with Scots pines and birch. A.A. Milne's loveable bear and friends had adventures in the copses, and played Poo Sticks from the little bridge over the river... If the Sussex High Weald Dairy had been in existance when the books were written perhaps Poo would have liked a little local Ricotta with his honey, or some fromage frais. Or even some Halloumi, sliced and grilled for breakfast.

The Dairy makes hard cheeses as well: Ashdown Foresters, made from organic cows milk, in an attractive circular shape with a basket-weave pattern on the surface, Duddleswell is made from sheep milk as is the delightfully named Slipcote, a soft cheese made to a recipe from Shakespeare's day when the name was self explanatory – 'slip' meaning a little piece, and 'cote' meaning cheese.

Below: How it's done. Hard work and professionalism ensure that each cheese is as good as the next at High Weald Dairy.

The following recipes were suggested by Mark and Sarah Hardy, who run the dairy – and eat lots of their own cheese!

Sussex Slipcote and turkey rolls

Preheat oven to Gas Mark 5/375F/190C. Sandwich the turkey escalopes or breast fillets between two sheets of wetted greaseproof paper on a sturdy chopping board and beat out with a rolling pin until about 1/2 in (10mm) thick. Spread the garlic and the Sussex Slipcote cheese over the turkey and season with the black pepper. Lay one bacon rasher and one apricot on top of each turkey escalope and sprinkle with the chopped mint. Roll the turkey breasts up neatly and tie securely with clean, thin string.

Heat the oil in a flameproof casserole and brown all parts of the turkey rolls. Pour in the stock or wine and bring to the boil. Cover and cook in the heated oven for 30 mins, or until the turkey feels tender and no pink juices ooze out when you push a fork into the rolls. During cooking, to keep the turkey moist, baste frequently with the stock.

Place the turkey rolls onto a heated serving dish, cover and leave to rest. Stir the yoghurt into the cooking juices and reheat without boiling. Pour into a warmed serving jug. Remove the string, cut the turkey rolls into thick slices and garnish with mint sprigs. Hand the sauce round separately. New potatoes and a crisp green salad are perfect accompaniments to this dish.

4 boneless turkey escalopes or breast fillets
2 cloves of garlic peeled and crushed
Freshly ground black pepper
4 rashers rindless back bacon
20 large mint leaves finely chopped
100g Herb and Garlic or Plain Sussex Slipcote soft cheese
4 ready to eat dried apricots
String for securing
200ml white wine, chicken stock or mixture of both
4 level tsp set yoghurt
Sprigs of fresh mint to garnish

All recipes serve 4 unless otherwise stated

Sussex Slipcote Pudding

Preheat oven to 170C
375g Plain Sussex
Slipcote cheese
60g ground almonds
40g candied peel
100g sugar
25g raisins
25g sultanas
4 egg yolks
Grated peel 1 lemon

Mash the Sussex Slipcote cheese. Add the sugar, ground almonds and egg yolks and beat until the mixture is creamy. Add the remaining ingredients, the candied peel, the raisins, the sultanas, and the grated lemon peel. Mix well. Place the mixture into a buttered deep ovenproof dish. Cook in the pre-heated oven for about 30mins. Serve this pudding hot or cold with crème fraiche.

All the rennet used by Sussex High Weald is vegetarian.

Above: Both Barrels fruit wines: Capturing the tastes of orchard and hedgerow, Both Barrels fruit wines from Horam in Sussex.

Next time you're looking for a wine to partner local cheese and fresh baked bread, why not try a glass of gooseberry? Back to **Both Barrels** in Horam, East Sussex who make a full bodied, medium dry gooseberry wine with an ABV of 12.5%. Served chilled, it not only goes very well with cheese, but compliments fish well, and makes a natural partner to grilled mackerel served with a gooseberry sauce.

Tasters of wines made with Cabernet Sauvignon or Shiraz grapes often refer to blackcurrant flavours, but Both Barrels make a real blackcurrant wine that is rich enough to substitute for Cassis in a Kir Royale – 1 measure blackcurrant wine to 5 measures champagne (or sparkling wine). It also makes an intriguing wine ice, simply freeze hard, beat at the last minute and serve in small stemmed glasses. There will still be liquid – nothing has been done to remove the alcohol – but the sensation of gritty ice crystals amongst the smooth liqueur flavour of blackcurrants is sensational – a spoonful of double cream or yoghurt turns it into a dessert.

Above: Always popular on a small scale because of their beauty and often feisty character, there is a growing interest in Rare Breed chickens for quality egg and meat production.

The following recipes come from Gina Burt, whose aptly named company, **Farmhouse Cookery** produces traditional cakes for top London stores and other fine food outlets. It's not surprising they are so successful, because their whole focus is quality and taste, so much so that they won the 'Great Taste Award' category of best traditional cake. To let you in on a secret, if you buy Harvey Nicols Orange and Lavender cake in a tin – then it came from the Burts' farm based kitchen.

All recipes serve 4 unless otherwise stated

Cheese Strada

125g Rindless British
back bacon
1 tsp olive oil
1 medium onion, peeled
and sliced
30-60g British butter,
softened
5-6 slices day-old bread
175g mature cheddar
cheese, grated
4 eggs – size 3
450ml single cream and
milk, mixed
1/4 level tsp chilli
powder
1 level tsp Merchant
Farmer's Sussex wine
mustard

This recipe is perfect for impressing breakfast visitors. Gina makes it the evening before, keeps it overnight in the fridge and puts it in the oven early in the morning.

Fry the bacon in the oil until lightly cooked. Remove from the pan and cut into pieces. Add the onion to the pan and fry until soft. Remove from the pan. Butter the slices of bread and cut them into cubes or triangles. Arrange half of the bread in the base of an ovenproof dish and sprinkle with half of the grated cheese. Top with the rest of the bread and the grated cheese. Scatter the fried onion and bacon over the top. Beat the eggs together with the cream and milk mixture, chilli and mustard. Pour over the ingredients in the dish and leave to stand for 30 mins, or put in the fridge overnight. Set the oven to moderately hot, gas mark 5/375F/190C, and bake for 45-60 minutes, or until firm. Note: This is a very flexible dish – you can leave out the bacon and add anchovies instead, or smoked haddock, or chunks of roasted onion.

Below: Growers pride. The kind of display you might see at a horticultural show, in the south-east, alongside the six foot leeks and the twenty pound cabbage. Admire the giants, but buy the smaller vegetables for flavour.

Pork fillets with figs and Taleggio cream

Soak figs overnight in wine with a sprig of rosemary. Drain figs, reserving the wine, removing the hard stalk from each one. Split the pork fillets open lengthways, cover with clingfilm and beat with a rolling pin until double their original width. Season. Cut 25g (1oz) cheese into 12 small dice; push a piece into each fig. Place ham down the centre of each fillet, arrange figs on top and fold over the ham. Reshape fillets; tie at intervals with fine string. Sit pork on the remaining rosemary sprig in a roasting tin just large enough to hold them and drizzle over the wine. Roast at gas mark 6/400F/200C for 30-35 minutes until just tender. Chop remaining cheese. Put in a saucepan with the butter and cream and melt over a low heat until blended. Season. Spoon a little cheese sauce over pork for the last 15mins of cooking. Cover remainder and keep warm just off the heat. Transfer fillets to a carving board. Cover with foil. Put roasting tin on hob and bring juices to the boil, bubble for 3-4 minutes until 45-60ml (3-4 tbs) liquid remains. Stir into the sauce. Serve with the pork.

12 ready to eat figs,
chopped
2 large sprigs fresh
rosemary
100ml white wine
Salt and ground black
pepper
2 British pork fillets
75g sliced Parma ham
225g Taleggio cheese
25g butter
284ml carton double
cream
Serves 6

Winchelsea, in Sussex, between Hastings and Rye, is a 'new' town, built in 1287 when the original Winchelsea was devoured by the sea. When the current Winchelsea was built it was a port, one of the five Cinque Ports of great importance on this coast, so close to France. Instead of trying to consume this new town, the sea retreated and it's now a mile from the sea, very quiet, almost eerily empty of people, but crammed with beautiful houses set off with crumbling town walls. There is an excellent butcher who sells delicious freshly baked pies, local lamb and speciality preserves.

Above: Magnificent joints of organic beef from Boathouse Farm in Sussex. You can buy direct from their farm shop, and see the tranquil farmyard at the same time, or from the organic section in major supermarkets.

Drive towards the sea and Winchelsea beach and you may notice a small white hut adorned with a red-and-white awning and the name **Suttons**. You may notice it because of its blackboard outside offering temptations such as Gresham duck, or local lobster or wood pigeon. A tiny Alladin's cave crammed full of local fish, gourmet fowl and occasional 'specials', it's a delightfully eccentric place to stock up on extras for a picnic. On a really special day, you might be shown the owner's ferrets!

Wood pigeons are often underrated – perhaps because they are cheaper than pheasant to buy. A juniper marinade will bring out their rich, gamey flavour and long, slow cooking will make even the oldest birds succulent and tender.

Pigeon pâté

3 pigeons
275ml red wine or sherry
Tbs olive oil
2 red onions
225g farmhouse sausagemeat
1 thick slice brown wholemeal bread
Seasonings:
1 bay leaf and black pepper for the marinade

For the pâté:
Black pepper
Salt – only if sausages are low in seasoning
Tsp fresh chopped thyme
Tsp tomato purée
Serves 8

Chop the pigeons into four pieces, then marinade in the wine/sherry, olive oil, chopped onions, bay leaf and black pepper. Put, covered, in the fridge for 2 days, turning occasionally. Take the pigeons out of the marinade, put the bread to soak in the liquid, remove the meat from the bones and chop into half very small, half larger slivers. Mash the bread well with a fork, mix it, and any remaining marinade, with the pigeon and sausage meat and season with the tomato purée, thyme, black pepper and salt if needed. Pack the pâté into two greased dishes – ideally long and thin – cover with foil, put in a baking dish with water to come half way up the dishes, and bake at gas mark 4 for 1 to 1 1/2 hours, or until a thin skewer inserted into the pâté comes out clean. Put to cool. Serve with crusty bread rolls or oatcakes. This pâté freezes well for up to a month.

Pigeons in the Pot

This is a wonderfully hearty winter meal, serve steaming in front of hungry guests – in a perfect world it could be cooked in a deep stewpan hung over a woodfire in a great inglenook fireplace. Without the woodsmoke for seasoning a small piece of smoked bacon or sausage adds an authentic tang.

4 pigeons
1 bottle robust red wine
275ml olive oil
4 fresh bay leaves
16 juniper berries
225g button mushrooms
4 cloves smoked garlic
110g pearl barley
225g piece of smoked bacon or sausage
Small glass of port
2 tbs redcurrant or sloe jelly

Wipe the pigeons and dry well, inside and out. Lightly crush the juniper berries, then put 4 berries inside each pigeon. Put the birds in a deep bowl, cover with the wine and oil, tuck in the bay leaves after crumpling them to release their flavour. Cover and leave in the fridge for 2 to 3 days, turning occasionally. Remove from marinade – saving the liquid, and drain. Meanwhile rinse and then boil the barley in water for 15 minutes, drain, rinse with cold water and drain again. Chop the button mushrooms into large pieces, mix them with the pearl barley and pack the mixture inside the birds, peel the garlic and put one clove into the barley. Put the pigeons in a deep casserole, pour over the marinade, tuck the bacon or sausage into the dish, add a generous seasoning of black pepper, cover and cook in a moderate oven gas mark 4/350F/180C for 2 hours, until the birds are very tender. Carefully lift the pigeons out, using a perforated spoon to drain them as you go, put them in a deep, hot serving dish and keep warm. Quickly heat the port in a saucepan, stir in the jelly and keep stirring as it dissolves, add the cooking juices and boil fiercely for 2 or 3 minutes until it reduces a little, spoon over the pigeons and serve.

If you are cooking over the fire then simply pour the port and jelly into the cooking pot and give a gentle stir before ladling the birds out into deep soup bowls. Serve with lots of crusty bread.

All recipes serve 4 unless otherwise stated

Above: Immaculate strawberry fields with the promise of a delicious harvest to come - look at the picture opposite for proof.

All recipes serve 4 unless otherwise stated

The several varieties of 'giant' strawberries that make their appearance in the shops in July make an unusual dessert if you carefully slice off a 'lid', hollow them out with a spoon and fill with ricotta cheese mixed with a sprinkling of macaroon biscuit crumbs. Put the lid back and dredge with caster sugar, serve with cream or ice-cream. What to do with the pulp you have left? For a palate sharpening 'starter' liquidise it with an equal volume of red currants, sieve, then use the tangy sauce to cover the base of a large serving plate. Make an arrangement of thinly sliced Mozzarella cheese in the centre of the sauce, top with small bunches of assorted salad leaves, including rocket if possible, lightly coated in olive oil. Lay a few strings of red currants over the leaves, top with wafer-thin shavings of strong, hard ewe's cheese and finish with a liberal grind of black pepper.

East Dean and Alfriston are fairytale villages with flint-walled cottages, gardens overflowing with hollyhocks and roses and, nearby, the Sheep Centre, in the Seven Sisters Park, named after the seven white cliffs overlooking the English Channel, where the tranquil River Cuckmere meanders its way to the cliff-edged beach. There, sea cabbage grows above the sea-line and, at sea, black shags dive for shoaling mackerel.

Above: Smoked pumpkin - guaranteed to intrigue.

The Seven Sisters Sheep Centre is in a magnificent complex of farm buildings set in fertile countryside freshened with the tang of the nearby sea. There are daily demonstrations of sheep milking, you can enjoy a sheep's milk ice cream, and choose from a selection of cheeses, or take home yoghurt or even some wool to spin. In season, you can watch the sheep being shorn.

Inland, in autumn, the fields at **Tulley's Farm** in West Crawley are dotted orange with **pumpkins**, as is the inside of the marquee they erect to show off their produce. If you like the unexpected, or have children who do,

then there's a witches 'grotto' with pumpkin lanterns to inspire you to create your own for Hallowe'en. There's a lot of flesh to scoop out of a big pumpkin, and some of them on show are really big, giant 'Sumo' ones that can reach up to 80lbs.

A continually increasing variety of pumpkins and squashes is appearing; a variety called Turkish Turban is so beautiful that it really does look as if it could be a hat – scooping out the shell and using it as a soup tureen is a more practical use for its beauty.

Smoked Pumpkin

Smoked pumpkin is real vegetable 'goodie'. Buy, or borrow, one of the small, hob-top smokers used by fishermen to smoke their catch.

Prepare the pumpkin, or even better, butternut squash, by cutting it into large wedges, removing the seeds, scoring deep into the flesh than painting it with olive oil, sprinkling with chopped fresh thyme and a little finely grated ginger. Hot smoke for 20-30 minutes, until tender, then allow to cool. The smoked pumpkin has a unique flavour, it makes an excellent vegetarian main course with rice and salad or could be used as a vegetable dish with meat. Any left-overs, chopped up, mixed with French dressing and served piled up on an avocado, make an unusual starter.

Opposite: High Weald Dairy cheese with its distinctive basket weave pattern: a thin slice quickly grilled on a piece of ciabatta, topped with a thick slice of beef tomato, a handful of olives and drizzled with oil could only be bettered by sprinkling a little torn basil on top.

All recipes serve 4 unless otherwise stated

Sweet Sunset

750g pumpkin flesh
500ml milk
100ml yoghurt
Generous pinch ground
ginger
Dessertspoon runny
honey
4tbs caster sugar
2 sprigs lavender

An intriguing dessert that will have guests guessing the main ingredient in the velvet smooth orange-coloured cream.

The day before making the dessert, take the lavender flowers from the stalk, place on small square of washed and dried muslin, or similar cloth, tie to make small bundle that will not come undone. Put sugar in screw topped jar, bury lavender bag in the sugar, seal jar, shake well.

Chop pumpkin flesh roughly, cover with milk in a saucepan and cook gently until quite tender but not mushy. This takes from 15-30 minutes depending on the age and variety of the pumpkin. Allow to cool, strain reserving the milk. Purée the pumpkin flesh in a liquidiser adding a little milk if necessary to make a smooth creamy 'fool', add the honey, stir well, taste and add more ginger to taste. Divide the pumpkin into 4 serving glasses and chill.

To assemble: Spoon chilled yoghurt onto the purée, sprinkle with the lavender scented sugar.

American research has found that the combination of pumpkin and lavender is the 'sexiest taste/smell of all'. Intriguing!

Above: The colours of the ingredients for Sweet Sunset bring the kitchen to life.

Cheeseboard:

Old Plaw Hatch – a modern British hard cow's cheese from Sharpthorne in West Sussex. *Rumbold's Rustic* – a semi soft cow's cheese from Billingshurst in West Sussex. *Lord of the Hundreds* – a modern British hard cow's cheese from Turners Cheeses at Stonehurst in East Sussex.

Right: Lurking beneath the leaves, an onion squash almost ready for picking. The 'onion' refers to its shape but it also fries very well cut in chunks in a pan full of white or red onions with generous olive oil - caraway seeds really 'lift' the tastes.

Opposite: Sweet Sunset

All recipes serve 4 unless otherwise stated

west country

Avon • Cornwall • Devon • Dorset • Gloucestershire • Somerset • Wiltshire

Oposite: Cream teas, a feast of flavours as well as one for the eyes.

The West Country image of cream teas and pasties has given way to Rick Stein's vision of thunderous seas and a cornucopia of fish, but cream is still a taste of the west and the pasty an essential part of windswept picnics.

Clotted cream, as made in the farmhouse, is creamy milk that has stood a while in a wide, shallow pan, been heated slowly until a thick yellow crust forms around the rim, then chilled and the top, crusty layer is taken off with a draining spoon. The Cornish variety of clotted cream tastes more intense, almost caramely compared to the paler Devonian variety, but both are wonderful with scones or 'splits' – light, yeast buns, and jam, or syrup or even treacle – the last combinations called 'thunder and lightening' by my West Country great-grandmother.

There seems to be an affinity between cream and cider in the west; many farm outlets sell both, such as Little Hayes on the London side of Exeter, where they offer ciders of varying sweetness and lots of thick cream.

Right: A barrel of farmhouse cider in Autumn, gently burbling and humming to itself in a quiet corner as the natural yeasts work. Winter comes, the murmuring ceases, and the golden liquid is ready to enjoy, each farm's offering as different as the apples it's made from.

Cornish curds and cream

600ml fresh milk
Tsp of lemon juice
Serves 2

Buying milk direct from the farm might well be the inspiration for trying this simple, but delicious dish. The dessert changes according to the breed of cows in the herd – Channel Island milk is extra rich, a deep cream, almost yellow in summer, whilst milk from Ayrshire cows is naturally homogenised, with a scarcely visible cream on the top. New flavours come from trying fresh goats' milk – almost coconut milk in taste, while ewes' milk yields masses of curds and very little whey – a reason why our ancestors used it so much to make cheese, and why there is such a growth in British ewe cheese development today.

Above: Pure, cool cow's milk in a jug and bowl made by the potter at the picture postcard village of Boscastle on the Cornish coast. Nearby dairy herds graze on fields enclosed by dry stone walls to protect them from the mighty Atlantic winds.

Add the lemon juice to the milk, heat very slowly – do not allow to boil. Take off the heat when curd forms. Lay a square of muslin in a sieve over a basin, pour slowly, or ladle the curd into the muslin and leave to drain for two hours in a cool place.

Serve the curds with clotted cream and fine ground vanilla sugar.

Fresh fish is plentiful and a visit to the picturesque Cornish harbour of Boscastle, on the north Cornish coast, can often yield freshly cooked **crab** – look for hand-painted signs beside the lobster pots outside the whitewashed cottages.

Crab sandwiches on the beach at Beer, on the softer, South Devon coast, are another West Country treat. The stoney beach seems out of an earlier age, with its beach huts and deck chairs and quiet sheltered cove, the shore slopes steeply and fishing boats are pulled up to one side to unload their catch, some of which is sold from a shop at the edge of the beach. Red Gurnard in summer is much prized by locals and visitors, at it's best simply baked in the oven and served with a squeeze of lemon

or lime, its firm white flesh ample reward for having braved the vicious spines along its back.

If you visit Beer when the **mackerel** are running you might like to hire a boat complete with lines and spinners and catch your own, or buy your fish, absolutely fresh and shining, from the shop.

Mackerel with Gooseberries

Some recipes stand the test of time. Serving a pyramid of shining, slivered fillets of rich tasting mackerel, with a sharp fruit purée as sauce, could well have been the very recent invention of an innovative chef. Instead it is an old West Country commonsense way of dealing with a naturally oily fish.

8 fresh mackerel fillets
225g gooseberries
10g butter
Black pepper

Wash, top and tail the gooseberries, cook them in just enough water to stop them sticking to the pan, or better still microwave them until just tender, add the butter. Purée the fruit in a food processor. Taste. If absolutely necessary add a touch of sugar, but not a lot, it should taste tart. Rinse and pat dry the fillets, season with freshly ground black pepper. Put the fillets under a grill pre-heated to hot and cook for 2-3 minutes, turning once. Serve the mackerel with the gooseberry sauce and tiny new potatoes dressed with crème fraiche – or, more traditionally, a spoonful of clotted cream.

Opposite: Mackerel on the beach; food as art.

Pasties, say some, are what made the West Country famous. When they used to be made to take down the mines, they often had two fillings in one package, sweet at one end, savoury the other, and the thick pastry edge was for dirty hands to hold and throw away, not to be eaten. Today, West Country pasties, like Ginsters, are a great success story and sold all over the country – and all of the pastry is eaten!

One bite tells you what you're eating. The Cornish Pasty is a regional speciality with a nationwide reputation.

Markets have always been a feature of life in the West Country. Twice-weekly markets in the long main street of antique-shop-crammed Honiton have now been joined by a Farmers' Market. Cullompton, too, and Plymouth are venues where producers bring their wares. Several farmers on Exmoor and Dartmoor now bring meat into town and are establishing regular customers who appreciate humane farming methods and the accompanying attention to standards and therefore quality.

Many years ago pannier markets were common, a farmer's wife would bring her dressed poultry, eggs and cream, perhaps a little butter and cheese. Since she travelled by horse-drawn cart her journey would necessarily be short in today's terms and fit in with the concept of as few food miles as possible. Farmers' Markets, the 'new' direct marketing, is a way forward with links to the past.

One such **beef** producer, 'Wild Beef', certainly has an attention-getting company name, and the quality of their product demands similar attention. 'Wild Beef' comes from the idyllic village of Chagford, on Dartmoor in Devon, where a remarkable pair of country 'gear' shops stand side by side and locals and tourists enjoy the comparisons of best 'green wellies' or hikers' rucksacks, or good kitchen china – the list is endless. But back to the beef…

The cattle are reared on Dartmoor and summer grazed on delicious, unimproved pastures scattered with wild flowers and dotted with bilberries. Richard Vines, 'Mr' Wild Beef, uses traditional grazing to bring the produce of his native breed animals to perfection, you might well see some of the herd on the National Trust headlands above Sidmouth.

His fans are united in praise of the beef, as in the following the quote from Gilly and Clive Redfern from the Turf Hotel, Exminster, published in the colourful 'Wild Beef' brochure: "We wouldn't serve our customers anything we wouldn't eat ourselves. We buy 'Wild Beef' because of its matchless quality and lack of wastage." The food writer, Phillipa Davenport in the *Financial Times,* wrote about a joint of 'Wild Beef' that she had cooked for Christmas lunch. 'It provided,' she said, 'a meal to remember.'

All recipes serve 4 unless otherwise stated

Fairings

110g butter
110g granulated sugar
110g golden syrup
225g plain flour
1/2 tsp salt
2tsp baking powder
2 tsp bicarbonate of soda
2 tsp mixed spice
3 tsp ground ginger
1 tsp ground cinnamon

Cornish Fairings are crunchy, spicy biscuits that used to be sold at 'hiring fairs' where dairy maids and other workers would find new employers, and 'hirer' and 'hired' alike might be tempted by the stalls of 'sweetmeats and fancies'. Today's Cornish Fairings sell to locals and tourists alike because of their unique taste. To make them at home you must move the baking trays from top to bottom of the oven half way through the cooking time, or bang the tray of half-baked biscuits so that the mixture spreads out and makes the traditional crackle top. Once baked they keep wonderfully in an airtight tin.

Sieve together all the dry ingredients. Rub in the butter until the mixture resembles breadcrumbs. Just melt the syrup then add it to mixture and mix in well. Make walnut sized balls, and roll them between the palms of your lightly floured hands, place them well apart on a lightly greased or non-stick baking sheet. Bake at the top of an oven preheated to gas mark 6 for 10 minutes then put down to a lower shelf replacing the top with a new batch, or take the tray out from the oven, give it a sharp rap on a kitchen counter – the biscuits will spread out and 'crack' and replace in the oven. Bake for a further 7 minutes or so until brown. Leave for a few minutes to firm a little and then remove with a spatula, cool on wire trays and finally store in an airtight tin.

The Devon coast to the east of Exeter has been a haven to the young Queen Victoria, an inspiration to the artist Sir John Millais, and a haunt of smugglers. Today, even at the height of the summer season there is a sense of calm, of tranquillity in the elegant Regency architecture of Sidmouth flanked by soaring sandstone cliffs, and the idyllic thatched cottages of Branscombe nestling in a green valley leading to the sea. A delicious mixture of harvest from the sea and the land makes itself felt in the foods on offer. If you enjoyed a crab sandwich on the beach at Beer on the first day of your visit, then perhaps on the next you could have fish and chips at the pub overlooking the beach – locally caught fish, and local potatoes, with a glass of local ale. Walk back up the main street, with the crystal-clear stream running beside you, for a West Country ice cream, or to buy a fruit wine – elderberry or sloe, or even birch sap, for sale alongside local fudge. A home made pasty, for supper, from the butcher, or a leg of local lamb, fattened on the grass scented with the sea breeze.

Below: Fresh eggs and butter from the farm, brown bread from the village baker, a fine West Country breakfast.

Opposite: Cornish Fairings.

The perfect place to eat a fresh baked **Cornish pasty** is in its own county, tucked into the shelter of a limpet strewn rock, the only additional condiment, salt spray from the rolling surf of an Atlantic beach.

The next best is – take your pick from the horsey delights of Badminton Cross Country Three Day Event, or the Devon County Agricultural Show, or the Bath and West… Fresh baked on site, but always made in Cornwall, the Cornish Pasty Co (Mobile) Ltd offers everything from the traditional 16oz chuck steak Cornish pasty to a 6oz children's pasty; they even do 'take-away' Cornish cream teas from their highly recognisable dark green units.

An important decision for many specialist food producers' year is how many '**shows**' to attend. There is a growing number of opportunities for small regional food producers to meet their market face to face. In the West Country, for example, the West Wilts Show attracts some 100,000 visitors over a three-day period, making it the largest show in the area. The Food and Drink marquees are a must for lovers of 'real' innovative food often produced to what we used to call good 'old fashioned' standards but are learning to realise are today's standards. The Royal Bath and West Show is another great hunting ground – the winners of the West Country food awards are announced there, and with entries such as Hot Smoked Duck Breast and Damson Gin, it's an opportunity to see how diverse 'local produce' can be.

In Cornwall, the **Budock Vean** is a golf and country house hotel, with its own golf course and walk, through towering palms, to a secluded beach on the Helford river.

It should be obligatory for visitors to the Helford to read Daphne Du Maurier's *Frenchman's Creek*. And to rent a little boat and sail, or row, quietly up one of the numerous creeks, perhaps even Frenchman's Creek itself, and imagine the pirate vessel, silently at anchor. If, while you are gently drifting with the tide, a haunting cry echoes from the densely wooded slopes, don't be alarmed – it's only the peacocks, where they strut on velvet lawns sheltered from the sea.

Two of the following recipes, given by the hotel, are full of fishy delights – the last uses the unique Cornish Yarg, a nettle wrapped cheese that's almost too attractive to eat. The dishes would be extra delicious cooked in a cottage overlooking water. There's a perfect one owned, and rented out for holidays by the National Trust, tucked down beside the rushing stream in the picturesque harbour village of Boscastle, where there's a shop to buy freshly landed fish up the hill, and the occasional fisherman bringing his catch into the tiny harbour.

Above: There was an old country custom of grazing a billy goat alongside dairy cows. The goat would, apparently, eat plants poisonous to the cows - hopefully they didn't harm the goat, especially handsome Golden Guernseys like this one.

Cornish Mouclade

Cook the shellfish accordingly, then drain the stock off each one. Sweat shallots and onions in a large saucepan until soft and colourless. Add garlic, curry powder, saffron, bay leaf, lemon juice, stock and wine, reduce by half. Beat the egg yolks and cream in a bowl, stir in a ladle full of the hot broth, then pour into the pan and simmer over a low heat for 5 minutes stirring occasionally. Do not let it boil. Add the cognac and the cayenne pepper and season. Then add the fresh herbs. Heat the shellfish in a steamer and ladle over the sauce.

12 clams
22 shrimps
12 baby langoustines
24 mussels
150ml white wine
1 bay leaf
1/2 chopped onion
25g butter
4 chopped shallots
2 cloves chopped garlic
2 tsp curry powder
2 pinches saffron
Juice 1 lemon
2 egg yolks
150ml double cream
2 splashes cognac
1 small pinch cayenne pepper
Fresh herbs – plenty of dill, parsley and tarragon

All recipes serve 4 unless otherwise stated

Tians of lightly cured river trout and avocado with a fresh tomato and basil dressing

400g trout fillet
110g smoked salmon
1 large garlic clove finely chopped
3 shallots finely chopped
1 1/2 tbs lemon juice
1/2 tsp salt
12 turns black pepper mill
Pinch cayenne pepper
Few drops Worcester sauce
2 small avocados
Mixed baby salad leaves to garnish

For the dressing:
2 fl oz extra virgin oil
1 tbs lemon juice
2 tomatoes, skinned, seeded and finely diced
1/2 tsp coarse sea salt
8 basil leaves very finely shredded
Few turns black pepper mill

Thinly slice the trout fillet and the smoked salmon, then cut them into strips about 5mm wide. Put them in a bowl with the garlic, shallots, 1 tablespoon of the lemon juice, salt black pepper, cayenne pepper and Worcester sauce and mix well together. Halve the avocados and remove the stone and peel. Cut each half into thin slices, then mix with the remaining lemon juice and a pinch of salt.

Place a 9cm poaching ring or plain pastry cutter in the centre of each of 4 large plates. Divide half of the trout and salmon mixture between the rings and lightly level the top; don't press the mixture down – you want it to be loosely packed. Cover each one with the avocado slices and then with the remaining trout mixture, lightly levelling the top once more. Carefully remove the rings.

Lightly stir the dressing ingredients together in a bowl. Arrange 4 small piles of the salad leaves around each tian. Using a teaspoon, spoon little pools of the dressing between the leaves and then serve.

Twice Baked Cornish Yarg Soufflé

Boil milk, sliced onions, nutmeg, black pepper and salt. Make a roux, add the grated Yarg and gently add the liquid, then add beaten egg yolks and mustard. Fold in stiff egg whites. Spoon into ramekin dishes and bake in a bain mairie for 20 mins. Allow to cool and rebake prior to serving.

3 free range large eggs
120g Cornish Yarg – nettle rind removed
35g butter
35g strong white flour
1.8-2.4ml full fat milk
2 tbs English mustard
1/2 a nutmeg, ground
Pinch salt and black pepper to taste
1 large onion
3 spring onions

Did you know? When Sir Walter Raleigh first brought potatoes back to England they were a fabulous novelty. They were grown for their flowers. These were worn as button-holes by courtiers, dudes and all followers of fashion. The tubers were discarded, thought of as poisonous.

This information was given by the Burts, founders of **Burts Potato Chips**, the smallest crisp producers in Britain. Most of their potatoes are sourced from local farms, and they use mainly the Saturna variety – although they have been known to venture out of county in quest of 'the ultimate spud'. The potatoes are hand-sorted, sliced into oil, hand-stirred, salted, seasoned and packed while still warm. Sounds – and tastes – fresh, crisp and just the thing to go with a glass of local cider.

Denhay Farms, in the lush Marshwood Vale near Bridport in Dorset, produce Farmhouse Cheddar, air dried ham and dry cured bacon. As they say, 'we use the traditional West Country cycle: we grow grass which cows eat to produce milk from which comes the Cheddar, and whey which is fed to the pigs which produce the muck which goes to grow the grass to feed the cows…'

Denhay Cheddar has won lots of prizes – it comes in the traditional rinded form, or a block and also the Dorset Drum, a 2kg cloth-wrapped cheddar. All are full of flavour and a tribute to West Country generations of cheesemakers.

Far left: A field of potatoes – a lot of crisps!

And now for something a little different! Their 'English prosciutto' is cured in apple juice and honey spiced with curing salts and herbs; it's then lightly smoked over wood chips and air dried for up to a year, and it tastes as good as it sounds. *A recipe suggested by Denhay:*

Pan roasted shallots with Denhay air dried ham

115g Denhay air dried ham
350g shallots
4 figs (optional)
55ml balsamic vinegar
55ml extra virgin olive oil
1 tsp brown sugar
1 tsp bay leaves
Salt and freshly ground black pepper
Thin salad leaves for garnish

Heat olive oil in a heavy saucepan, stir in the shallots, cover and cook over a medium heat for 5 minutes. Add the brown sugar, thyme, salt and pepper and 2 tbs water. Cover the pan and cook slowly over a slow heat, stirring the onions from time to time to prevent them sticking to the pan, for about 30 minutes or until the liquid caramelises slightly and the onions are soft with a little colour. Then add the vinegar, stir well and remove it straight away from the heat and allow to cool. This can be prepared in advance. Just before you are ready to serve, preheat the oven to gas mark 4/350F/180C and place the onions in a shallow, lidded casserole for 15mins. Arrange the ham on individual plates, lay the onions on the ham and pour the juices round the plate. Cut figs in four and arrange with the onions and garnish with salad leaves. Serve with good fresh bread and some Denhay butter.

Above: Air dried ham from Denhay, perfectly made and packed, waiting to be enjoyed just as it is, or wrapped around a succulent piece of monkfish, baked in the oven and served on a bed of puréed potatoes and celeriac seasoned with sea salt and a dash of balsamic vinegar.

It must be something about the air in Bridport, but not only is there Denhay producing cured products, but nearby **Todd Sadler** makes Bresoala, pastrami and two types of corned beef all from English beef. As well as his established products – and as for the corned beef, it's nothing like the corned beef that comes out of a can; it is dark, with an intriguing taste of spice – Todd and his team like to experiment. They're into Biltong –

all kinds of it, including fish. Then there are the smoked eggs, and all sorts of smoked fish at the Good Food Lovers Emporium.

Having begun the chapter with a fleeting reference to Rick Stein's wonderful descriptions of sea, and fish and stunning scenery – and above all flavour – in the West, his restaurant at Padstow, at the mouth of the River Camel, in Cornwall, continues to do wonderful things with the freshest fish. Then there's his bakery and delicatessen where all the bread is home made, as are the chutneys and marmalades – and you can order a sea food thermidor or fish pie to take away.

Below: Their own shells make admirable dishes on which to serve the scallops, roughly chopped, fried quickly in a little butter, with a sprinkling of fresh breadcumbs to absorb the juices in the pan, seasoned well with black pepper, lemon juice and fresh chopped parsley.

Cheeseboard:

Blissful Buffalo a soft white buffalow cheese from Panryn in Cornwall. *Campscott Original* a modern British hard ewe cheese from Ilfracombe in Devon. *Quickies Traditional Oak Smoked Cheddar* a speciality hard cow's cheese from Exeter in Devon.

All recipes serve 4 unless otherwise stated

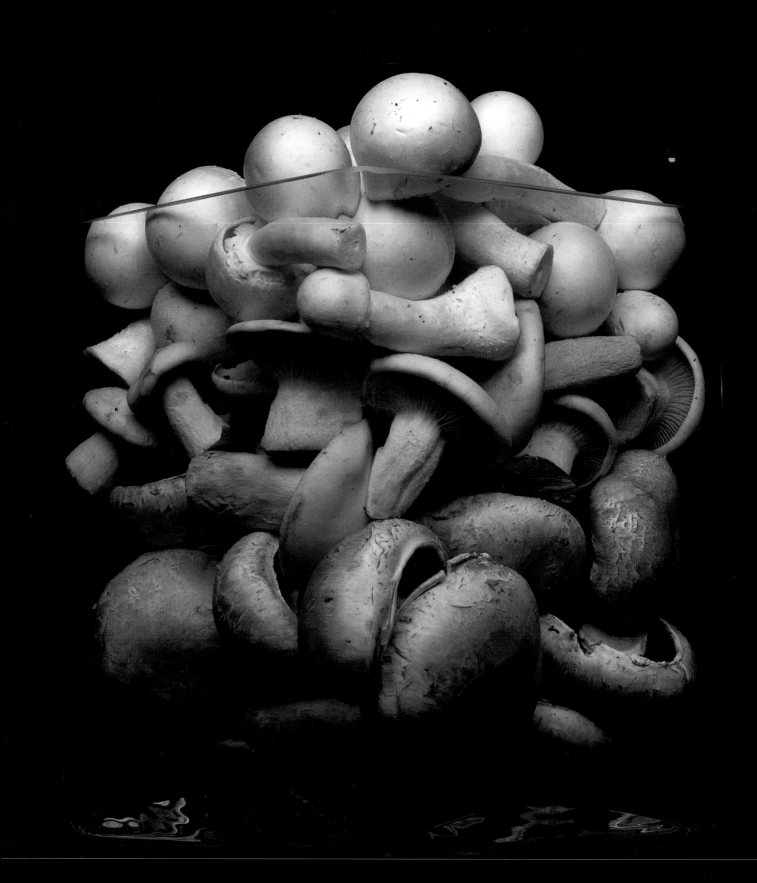

hampshire &

Hampshire • Oxfordshire • East Gloucestershire

cotswolds

As a county Hampshire has much to offer – the New Forest – hunting place of kings; yachting at Lymington; the great docks of Southampton and Portsmouth; the city of Winchester with the magnificent cathedral and bustling market; world famous chalk streams for trout fishing and watercress; the Roman Old Sarum at Salisbury.

The richness of the area is reflected in the foods it produces. The fine wines of the Meon Valley vineyard are produced from grapes grown on the chalk downs, their sparkling wine is a cool delight. A drive towards Portsmouth takes you to **George Gale & Co**, a family brewery since 1847 who offer guided tours finishing in the gift shop where you can buy their brews, including the award winning Festival Mild. You will inevitably have passed some of their pubs on your route as they have over 100 in the area. The route to the New Forest from Portsmouth takes you close to the **Chalcroft Farm Shop** where they sell their own recipe venison sausages and the 'Hampshire sausage'.

The abundance of venison products on offer in local butchers and delicatessens is a constant reminder of the New Forest. The great beech trees, splendid at any time of year, give dappled shade in spring, form a cool retreat in a burning June, and structure to a secret, silent place in snow. Often unseen, great numbers of deer live here as well as game birds – pheasant and partridge – and everywhere, the independent-minded ponies.

A picnic in the New Forest allows you time to take in the stillness, to enjoy a sense of timelessness and to imagine the cacophony of sounds the long past royal hunt would have brought into such stillness. Hunting game was not only an entertainment but also a way to furnish the great houses with meat. The Tudor

Opposite: Wood blewitt farmed in Hampshire: its taste, like its appearance here, can be distinctly theatrical. Cook with a dark, full-bodied wine, season with Sechuan pepper and salt, thicken the resulting sauce with arrowroot - curtain up!

Above: Fresh trout from the chalk streams, catch, gut, and cook instantly in a splash of oil after only the briefest of washes, for maximum taste.

aristocracy used the quality and variety of the food they dispensed to highlight their importance. Presentation was calculated to impress, ornamental fowl were cooked and then displayed in full plumage, banquets were meticulously planned, all sorts of marzipan 'conceits' constructed by clever cooks to please their masters. The **Portland sheep** – a ginger-legged breed with swept back horns and originating from the Isle of Portland, not far from the Hampshire border – was much sought after in Tudor times for the quality of its meat. Today, as a breed, it is just recovering from near extinction. It is becoming a success story for the Rare Breed Trust, and the few stalwart breeders who persevered to increase flock numbers. The meat has become so sought after through the butchers licensed to sell Rare Breed produce, that it is very much a case of demand outstripping supply.

Right: The Portland Down, a rare breed sheep recovering from near extinction. As well as benifitting from the Rare Breed Survival Trust's butchers initiative, the efforts of a producer of Portland wool products are boosting the breed's profile.

The following two recipes for using sheep's milk were given by Olivia Mills, who lives in Hampshire and is proprietor of **Brebilait Products**, with the memorable catch line: 'Fresh from ewe to you'. Many years ago I bought her excellent book on sheep milking and followed the recipes it contained to make delicious sheep milk cheese and yoghurts. My son is following in my footsteps, using the now 'well-thumbed' copy. Which goes to show what an investment a good book can be!

All recipes serve 4 unless otherwise stated

American-style breakfast pancakes

Very delicious pancakes, not necessarily known in the USA, but a great favourite in Hampshire.

Sift all the dry ingredients into a large mixing bowl, measure the milk in a big jug and add eggs and yoghurt and beat well. Mix with dry ingredients and whisk to form thick batter. Heat a large frying pan over a medium heat, add a bit of butter and put in pancakes by the tablespoonful. Do not let them spread. When the bubbles rise, flip over. When cooked serve with maple syrup.

315g plain flour
1 tbs caster sugar
2 tsp cream of tartar
1 tsp bicarbonate of soda
1 tsp salt
2 large eggs
230ml British sheep yoghurt
230ml local sheep milk

Crême Caramel au lait de Brebis

90g granulated sugar
3 tbs water
600ml local sheep milk
4 eggs
1 tsp vanilla essence

This recipe is famous in the area of Millau on the Tarn but is equally delicious in Hampshire

To make the caramel, melt the sugar in a heavy saucepan, stirring all the time. When it becomes light brown take off heat and add water, stir well. Beat eggs into milk, add vanilla and pour over caramel in pie dish. Place in a bain marie in a medium oven and cook until firm, about 1 hour. When cool, ease round edges and turn out onto a serving dish.

Opposite, left: Fennel is highly decorative in this Hampshire field, its delicate fronds fluttering in the lightest breeze, using the feathery leaf as a garnish turns hard boiled eggs with mayonnaise into a feast for the eyes as well as the palate. The crunchy 'bulb' of the plant adds a feisty aniseed taste as well as crunch to salads.

Fundamentally Fungus would like to take you on a gastronomic adventure. The subtle scent of autumn woodlands is creeping into hotel, pub and restaurant menus across the South of England – all year round! If you are tempted by an offering of native Wood Blewitt then you don't need to feel guilty about destroying a delicate woodland environment if the fungi in question were grown by Jane Dick and her team at Meon Hill in Hampshire. By using high specification growing rooms they produce these otherwise seasonal delicacies all year round. They also produce the slow growing Japanese Shitake and are working with other speciality growers to meet the British demand for speciality mushrooms.

There are a growing number of exciting varieties of fungi on offer to enterprising chefs: chestnut mushrooms – often called Brown Caps or Portabella mushrooms – horse mushrooms, wood blewitts and oyster mushrooms, and no-one had to go out into the woods to gather them. Most importantly, you know exactly what you're eating! No Agatha Christie type misidentifications. There are other delights, Japanese and Asian varieties such as Shitake, Maitake, Shimeji, Enoki, Pink and Yellow Oyster and Paddy mushrooms.

Below: Focus on fungus.

Wood blewit *(lepista nuda)*

Wild wood blewits appear during the second half of autumn and into the winter. They can be found growing in several different habitats – mixed woodland, hedgerows, even in gardens. At times there are a lot of them but bearing in mind the decimation that has happened to many woodland fungi where they've been gathered commercially, it's very good news that they are now being grown specifically for the table. The gills of a wood blewit are a beautiful lilac colour, as they get older they become paler, but never go brown. If you take a spore print – leave the cap, gill side down on a piece of white paper for a few hours – it will turn pale pink. They smell perfumed, and are sometimes used in desserts, or preserved in spiced alcohol (when they should be kept in the fridge). You can also preserve them in good olive oil, or wine

All recipes serve 4 unless otherwise stated

vinegar, but they must always be thoroughly cooked before eating, and as some people are allergic to them – always try a little if you are eating them for the first time, and warn guests what they will be eating. Wood blewits have a strong flavour, and will add robustness to meat or vegetable stews even when used in small quantities. One of the best ways to discover their unique flavour is to cook them with onions, as in the following recipe:

110g Fundamentally Fungus wood blewits
450g white onions
2 leeks
600ml full cream milk
75g butter
25g flour
1 tbs olive oil
Salt, pepper and ground nutmeg (optional)
4 crusty rolls

Clean the mushrooms by wiping the caps and cutting off the stems, chop into large pieces. Peel and slice the onions thickly. Wash the leeks well, drain and cut into inch long chunks – including the green. Melt 50g of the butter in a deep frying pan, add the onions and leeks, cook gently until just soft, then add the mushrooms and cook for at least 20 minutes, until all is well cooked and soft. Cut a 'lid' off the top of the rolls and pull out the soft bread inside – drop onto the moving blades of a blender, and whizz for a few seconds to make fresh breadcrumbs. In a separate pan, melt the remaining butter, add the flour to make a roux, add the milk and stir whilst bringing to the boil, when just boiling tip into the vegetable mixture and gently simmer until all is thick. Meanwhile crisp the roll 'cases' in the oven – you can paint the inside with a little butter or oil and sprinkle with a few chopped herbs before putting them in the oven if you like. Quickly fry the breadcrumbs in the olive oil. Season the mushrooms to taste with salt and pepper and add ground nutmeg if you like it.

To assemble: Put the rolls on warm plates, fill them with the mushroom mixture, top with crisped breadcrumbs. Serve with a hearty red wine, a crisp salad dressed with a herby salad dressing.

All recipes serve 4 unless otherwise stated

Mushroom Supper

A delicious oven-baked dish, rich with mushrooms and cheese, complete with potatoes – it's a meal in itself.

Peel, wash and dry the potatoes, slice them thinly then wash and dry again. Rub a shallow baking dish with garlic then spread it with 1oz of the butter. Peel and chop the onions. Make layers of vegetables in the dish, starting with the potatoes, then the mushrooms, and ending with potatoes. Sprinkle each level with some chopped onions, a little butter, the parsley and, in all about half of the cheese, to come within an inch of the top of the dish. Sprinkle over the remaining cheese, pour over the cream, dot with the butter and then bake in a slow oven – gas mark 3/325F/170C for one and three-quarter hours, until it is bubbling hot and the potatoes are cooked – test with a skewer. The smell of this cooking will guarantee hearty appetites so it might be a good idea to serve it with hot crusty bread to mop up the delicious sauce.

1.15kg potatoes
1.15kg mushrooms
Clove of garlic
175g butter
175g crumbly cheese such as Lancashire
2 onions
Half a pint of double cream
Tbs chopped fresh parsley

Opposite: Mushroom supper – the finished article.

Below: Mushroom supper cooking in the pan.

Above: Hampshire Fare, a collection of specialist food products from all over the county.

Speciality food producers like their wares to be appreciated and sometimes band together to promote marketing. One such group, led by the enthusiastic Susanne Austin, is the **Cotswold Food Group**. With a farming background, Suzanne is a fervent believer in the quality of Cotswold produce, and her later retail and marketing experience has been invaluable in keeping the group attention focused on today's consumer-led marketplace.

Early members of the group include: Jonathan Crisp, 'Crisp by name, crisp by nature'. These crunchy crisps have eye-catching packets, dressed in jackets and ties. The rather grand looking sea salt and pepper variety come in 'black tie' with a bow tie, dress shirt and black jacket. Cheddar and spring onion sports a jaunty polka dot tie, and so on. Made at Oxford, under licence from a Canadian company, they are still very much a British product using local potatoes. Made in small batches, stirred by hand and cooked in 100% non hydrogenated peanut oil, they are made from unpeeled potatoes to preserve the natural vitamins and minerals. Ideal for 'dunking' in soft dips, they're seasoned with totally natural ingredients

Shaken Oak Farm originates from the 15th century. At the edge of the Cotswolds, it is on the route used by Charles I on his escape from Oxford in 1644. Its beginnings may be well in the past, but a recent innovation is the making of mustard there. The following recipe, from Shaken Oak, is a good way of enjoying one of their coarse grain mustards and really does justice to the taste of a prime piece of British beef.

All recipes serve 4 unless otherwise stated

Roast beef with mustard and peppercorn crust

900-1350g beef topside
joint
1 tbs crushed black
peppercorns
3 tbs Shaken Oak
mustard with garlic
2 tbs chopped parsley
1 tsp olive/vegetable oil
20g breadcrumbs

Place the joint on a trivet in a roasting dish. Press the crushed peppercorns over the joint. Open roast in a pre-heated oven gas mark 4/350F/180C for a calculated time (25 minutes per 450g) minus 15 minutes. Mix together the mustard, parsley and oil. Spread the mix over the surface of the joint and then press the breadcrumbs into mix. Return to the oven for final 15 minutes until the breadcrumbs are golden. Remove the joint from the oven and let the joint stand for 10 minutes before carving.

Another great partner for mustard is a good sausage. **J.W. Harman**, butchers at Milton Under Wychwood, offer a Cotswold sausage – pork, lemon and chives, it is, they say, 'a scholar amongst sausages' – and then there's the Champion Harman sausage, 'a quintessential pork sausage based on an original recipe by Grandad Harman incorporating a blend of spices and herbs that produces a sausage like a taste of yesteryear'. You can buy fresh baked bread from the Harmans and a fine selection of cheeses – and home baked pies and, of course, some mustard.

Above: Ready to make a crust for roast beef or baked ham, Wholegrain Mustard.

Cheeseboard:

Bridewell – a fresh cow's cheese or *Chandler's* – a semi-soft cow's cheese.

Below: These 'Corn Crows' are intended to scare birds from the growing number of domestic organic vegetable plots. After all, if you go to the effort of growing the finest tasting vegetables, it should be you who enjoys them.

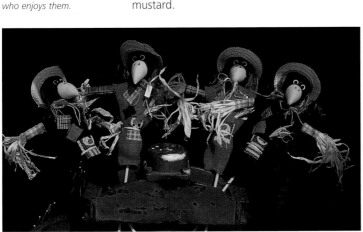

All recipes serve 4 unless otherwise stated

wales

The smallest city in Britain is St Davids, on the south-west coast of Wales, named after the patron saint of Wales. A visit to see the exquisite cathedral that gives the city its status is only one reason to drive to the west coast. The light is fantastic, clear and invigorating, changing to lowering and menacing in a moment. Its special lucidity has long attracted artists – John Knapp Fisher is one whose watercolours capture the fleeting shafts of light touching aged cottages. Prince Charles, Prince of Wales, has one of his paintings, a tribute perhaps to their capacity to capture an essence of the area.

St Davids' few shops offer a wide taste of the area. There is a baker who bakes pastries, sweet and savoury, all fragrant and gilded. The butcher offers leek-flavoured sausages as well as lean, small legs of tender Welsh lamb. There are local cheeses on offer, just right for a picnic on the nearby white sands. Back to the bakers for a restorative apple pie after a bracing – even in high summer – swim in the mighty Atlantic.

Up the coast for a search for **Sewin**, not always successful but when it is, a special treat because Sewin – the sea trout that is still fished for with long nets in the shallows of a rushing tide – has a fineness and flavour that captures the sea. The fish shops that offer the best chance of Sewin have another special – **laverbread** (or you might find it in a local market). A kind of seaweed that has been eaten for centuries, laverbread is sometimes fried in small cakes for breakfast or, as the cookery writer, Jane Grigson, suggested, added at the last minute to a vegetable soup – all ways of enjoying a boost of natural iodine. Welsh **beef** is eaten with a patriotic fervour by Welshmen at home and abroad and it's well worth their passion – properly hung by a good butcher it is the quality of meat that lifelong memories are made of.

Opposite: Placid fields overlooked by the hills of Wales, a perfect environment for Welsh sheep.

Below: A simply beautiful presentation for the simply beautiful quality of Welsh lamb.

Welshcakes are everywhere, in tea shops, in bakers, at fairs and fetes. At the annual coracle races on the magnificent River Teifi, local ladies bring plates of their own Welsh cakes to sell and in the best tradition of regional specialities everyone seems to have their own recipe and the visitor who can buy them might, or might not, get told the 'secret' ingredient.

There is a great tradition of cooking **cockles** in Wales. They've been served fried with a little bacon for breakfast, or pan fried with breadcrumbs and chopped spring onions: fry the breadcrumbs until crisp in a little oil and butter, add the cockles, put a lid on – the cockles jump! Shake the pan for a few minutes until hot and tasty, sprinkle with the spring onions and serve. Cockles are also delicious with pasta, even Italian restaurants serving them instead of the more traditional clams as a Marinare sauce.

Organic produce abounds in Wales, fruit and vegetables, cheese and meats, all produced without additives and to the high standards that go hand in hand with caring farming.

Below: These simple fishing nets are designed to be strung up across an estuary mouth when the tide is out so that the rising/retreating water does the rest . Despite being one of the earliest designs known to man they're too effective and now banned in many areas.

Party, party!

*The following recipes – to cater for special occasions – were given by Peter Jackson, team manager of the **Welsh National Culinary Team** at Hotel Maes-y-Neuadd, Talsarnau, Near Harlech, North Wales. The hotel is in an idyllic setting, nestling into a wooded mountainside with views across the Snowdonia National Park. This gracious old house has been sympathetically restored to provide a really luxurious haven, and as for the food… just read the recipes, and remember that they also make 'comestibles for the discerning', preserves and flavoured oils using the produce of their own kitchen garden and a harvest from the surrounding hedgerows.*

Potted fresh and smoked salmon

Beat the butter until light and airy. Fold in both salmons, chives and flavour with other ingredients. Chill for 24 hours

Toss the salad, sippets and French beans and place a little pile in the middle of the plate. Quenelle the salmon (shape like a narrow egg using two tablespoons) and place on top of salad. Garnish with melba toast. Pour dressing round salad and dot with vinegar.

Opposite, below: Capturing the essence of summer - sprigs of scented herbs and flowers soaking in an assortment of vinegars. Lavender in cider vinegar, to add zest to a fruit salad - or to dab on your wrists on a scorching hot day. Rose petals in raspberry vinegar to add magic to a rice pudding - or to dab behind your ears!.

1.8kg cooked fresh salmon, flaked
1.5kg diced smoked salmon
1.2kg unsalted butter
Horseradish
Lemon zest and juice
Tabasco
200g finely chopped chives
Salt
To finish
Various salad leaves
Sippets
Diced French beans, blanched and marinated in coarse mustard dressing
Melba toast
Natural herb yoghurt dressing
Reduced Balsamic vinegar
Serves 60 people

Salt marsh and mountain lamb with punchmep, Welsh potato cake and a cabbage parcel

60 salt marsh lamb cutlets
60 mountain lamb noisettes
1kg chicken mousse
200g laverbread
Crepinette
Salt and pepper
For the sauce:
3 litres brown lamb stock
1 bottle Madeira
200g finely diced shallots
2 bunches thyme finely chopped
100g unsalted butter
Serves 60 people

Season one side of the noisettes and seal in hot oil, remove without cooking second side. Mix the laverbread and mousse, check seasoning. When cold spoon some mousse on top of cooked side and cover with crepinette. Season bottom side and cutlets and seal in hot oil. Finish cooking in oven and then rest.

Sweat off the shallots and thyme in a little butter. Deglaze with Madeira and reduce by half. Add stock and reduce, check seasoning and monte au beurre

Punchmep

Combine all vegetables in a pan and crush, add butter and check seasoning.

1kg cooked carrots
1kg cooked swedes
500g cooked parsnip
500g cooked celeriac
400g unsalted butter
Seasoning

Cabbage Parcel

Steam the shredded cabbage in a pan with a little water. Add the cream and oatmeal, check seasoning, cool. Line a ladle with cling film, then a leaf, stuff with cabbage mixture and form a ball. Steam to reheat

Blanched Savoy cabbage leaves
Shredded cabbage
Double cream
Seasoning
Oatmeal

Potato Cake

Beat all the ingredients together, roll out and cut, cook on a griddle until hot.

3kg cooked potato
200g unsalted butter
200g flour
Salt and pepper

Finishing
Place the cabbage parcel at the back middle with punchmep and potato cake either side, then the cutlet and Noisette and surround with sauce.

Bara Brith mousse with elderflower ice cream

Whisk the egg yolks with sugar until white, boil the milk and pour over mixture and whisk. Return to a clean pan and cook until it coats the back off a spoon, do not boil. Strain, cool. Fold cream into custard. Cut the Bara into very small pieces and sprinkle with brandy then fold into mixture and pour into moulds, chill until firm. Unmould and dust with icing sugar.

2kg Bara Brith
30 egg yolks
2.5 litres milk
500g caster sugar
500ml brandy
35 leaves of gelatine
2.5 litres whipped double cream
Serves 60 people

Elderflower ice cream

12 egg yolks
500ml milk
500ml elderflower
cordial
250g caster sugar
200ml whipped double
cream
50g orange zest
To finish
Soft fruits
Brandy snap baskets
Sabayon
Mint

Whisk the yolks and sugar until white, boil the milk and elderflower and pour over the mixture, whisk. Return to a clean pan and cook until it coats the back of a spoon, do not boil. Strain. Chill quickly and stir in zest and whipped cream. Pour into ice machine and freeze.

Place mousse on plate, brandy snap basket close with fruits. Coat fruits with sabayon and ball ice cream into baskets garnish with mint.

The Welsh National Culinary Team was founded in 1993. They've travelled from Tywyn to Tokyo, from London to Luxembourg to promote the quality of Welsh food and drink, and the professionalism, touched with Celtic genius, has won them 77 international food medals from major competitions all over the world.

Welshcakes

900g Plain flour
2 tsp baking powder
1 tsp mixed spice
450g unsalted butter
350g caster sugar
225g currants
4 eggs
Milk

Sift the flour, baking powder and mixed spice, rub in butter. Add the sugar, currants and eggs. Mix in milk to make a soft dough and roll out to 1/4" (5mm) thick. Cut in small rounds and bake on hot griddle. Dust in sugar.

Very often, if you book a **holiday cottage** in Wales you will arrive to a tray full of home-made 'goodies'. We've had Welshcakes that were light, with a subtle, smokey taste from the griddle and still warm – and a comment from the young daughter of the house that her 'Mam' was so busy baking them for visitors that she never made them for the family! A different cottage and another welcoming tray, again with Welshcakes, and

home-made gooseberry jam – and delicious onion bread with fresh butter to enjoy with it. And a tale of almost failed endeavour. The onion bread was a favourite recipe which our hostess thought might get her a special mention in the tourist brochure, so it was served up, as our tray had been, to the tourist board inspector. He spread the very oniony delight with the very sweet jam – and pronounced it 'unusual'. She was too embarrassed to tell him he should have eaten it with the butter – but fortunately the quality of her Welshcakes salvaged the situation.

Leeks are a wonderfully versatile vegetable, and also very handsome, so it is not surprising that Welshmen delight in flourishing them at sporting events – especially when their opponents are English!

Above: Good bread, as baked in many Welsh farms and villages, is an essential. What would smoked salmon be without thinly sliced brown bread? How could you have cucumber sandwiches without a fine grained white loaf - how could you make bread pudding?

All recipes serve 4 unless
otherwise stated

First leeks

8 'baby' leeks
1 lemon
Good pinch seasalt
Black pepper
1/4 head of fennel
230ml yoghurt
3 eggs
tsp good olive oil
Small bunch flat leaf
parsley

A delicately flavoured starter or light lunch dish for the end of August, to celebrate the first of the British leeks. Hot tomato bread is a good accompaniment.

Split the leeks from the green end to just into the white, rinse them thoroughly under running water. Put the juice of the lemon, and a few shreds of the pithless peel into a deep frying pan, add the salt, a good grind of pepper, the fennel cut into vertical strips and the olive oil, lay in the cleaned leeks, add water to just cover and poach them gently until they are just tender – about 15 minutes. Leave the leeks to cool in the liquid.

For the sauce: separate the eggs, putting the yolks into a heatproof bowl with the lemon juice and put the whites to one side. Stir the yoghurt well, then add it to the egg and lemon, put the bowl over a pan of boiling water and cook, stirring, until the sauce has thickened – about 15 minutes, leave to cool. Meanwhile poach the egg whites in a little water, when firm drain them well, chop into thick shreds and put to cool.

To assemble: drain the leeks well, first by gently squeezing them then dabbing with kitchen paper. Put them on a serving dish, spoon over the sauce and sprinkle with the chopped egg white and roughly torn flat-leafed parsley.

Right: Comfort food after a walk by a wild Welsh sea, whole onions baked in the oven and finished with a knob of butter, serve hot. Or omit the butter, leave to cool, skin and dress with olive oil and a dash of balsamic vinegar.

Left: Baby leeks, leave them to grow bigger, or pull them at this size and fry gently in good Welsh butter, season with a grating of nutmeg and serve with wholemeal rolls and a glass of beer.

Pan fried leeks

A versatile dish that can be served hot or cold, on its own or with dry cooked fish or meat, or even topped with a poached egg. Its robust flavour seems to intensify if kept overnight in the fridge before eating.

Trim leeks of any damage, slit in half lengthways and rinse well under running water, cut into 5cm chunks. Put the olive oil in a deep frying pan, add the leeks, crushed garlic, bay leaves – crumple them in your hand before adding them, it releases more flavour. Cook gently for 20 minutes, until the leeks are just tender. Add the tomatoes, cut into 1/8ths, cook for a further 5 minutes. Put on serving dish, squeeze over the juice of half the lemon and some shredded peel, season with sea salt and pepper. Serve hot or cold. It's extra delicious served on toasted rye bread – perhaps topped with a slice of goat's cheese?

900g maincrop leeks – middle sized ones are best, the really big ones can be too mild.
450g tomatoes – vine tomatoes are tastiest
2 fat cloves of garlic
1 lemon
75ml olive oil
2 fresh bay leaves
Sea salt
Black pepper

All recipes serve 4 unless otherwise stated

Wales offers excellent quality poultry, from butchers and markets, and sometimes at the farm gate. The following recipe uses a good, farmhouse cider to complement the quality of both ingredients.

Chicken in Cider

1.35-1.8kg free range chicken

1 pt farmhouse cider

2 dessert apples (coxes are especially delicious)

1 onion

Tied bunch of fresh herbs – tarragon, flat-leaf parsley and thyme

25g butter

25g flour

Salt and pepper

A free range chicken has flavour, enhancing that flavour with farmhouse cider, apples and fresh herbs makes a memorable dish.

Wash and dry the chicken and put it in a deep casserole with the herbs. Core and chop the apples, leaving the skin on. Peel and slice the onion thickly, then tuck the apple and onion round the chicken. Pour over the cider. Cover closely and cook in an oven preheated to gas mark 6/400F/ 200C for 2 hours, until the chicken is very tender. Take the bundle of herbs out of the casserole, then, using a slotted spoon, lift out the chicken and put it on a hot, deep serving dish. Melt the butter in a saucepan, add the flour, whisk in the hot strained stock, as soon as it has thickened tip in the cooked apple and onion, stir gently then pour over the chicken.

Traditionally potatoes would have been eaten with a dish like this, but pasta is lighter and very good with a little of the sauce stirred into it before serving, then a leafy salad with a sharp French dressing.

Above: Quick to cook, quail, like these in Wales, work well with a fruity sauce, made at its simplest by cooking the poultry with a few quartered dessert apples and a glass of cider - Russet are especially good - when the meat is tender, mash the apples into the cooking juices.

Above: Cheese from Wales, slowly maturing to perfection.

Opposite: Pan fried leeks.

Cheeseboard:

Remarkable Valley - a modern British hard cow's cheese from Teifi Farmhouse Cheese in Dyfed. *Ba'a Bright* - a modern British hard ewe's cheese from Llandrindod Wells. *Caldy Abbey Cheese* - a cow's milk cheddar from Caldy Abbey, Caldy Island, Dyfed.

All recipes serve 4 unless otherwise stated

anglia

Bedfordshire • Cambridgeshire • Essex • Hertfordshire • Norfolk • Suffolk

If you are a fan of shellfish, then Leigh on Sea is a step back into another era with the bonus of cockles brought in daily from the nearby Maplin Sands and mountains of cockle shells behind the huts where they are prepared. The jellied eels and other fishy temptations draw a constant stream of visitors from nearby Southend with the longest pier in the world and over 100 acres of gardens to attract anglers as well as holiday makers – the first hope to catch big cod, the second to eat them!

Burnham on Crouch is a magnet for yachtsmen, its elegant Georgian buildings built when the town was a hive of shellfish trade; now it caters mainly for weekenders. Maldon, on the Blackwater, is famous for sea salt. On the edge of the river smart black weatherboarded warehouses are home to the Maldon salt company. The river itself is home to several 17th-century Thames barges, handsome red-sailed vessels that in summer can often be seen racing majestically.

Colchester was the first major Roman settlement in Britain – they came for the oysters. Visit in October when the quality of the local oyster is celebrated with a festival - it's a month with an 'r' in it so the shellfish will be at their best (the summer months. when there are no 'r's are when the oyster is

reproducing and tends to turn a dull, greyish black colour).

The father of the painter John Constable was the miller of Flatford Mill. This is the beautiful country that Constable painted, much of it as it was in his day, peaceful and unspoilt. Peace might not be a word that

Above: This way to culinary delights!

Opposite: Harvesting sugar beet in Anglia. The resulting harvest of sugar will make jams and preserves, fudges and biscuits... sweet!

Below: Tiptree preserves, instantly identifiable by their distinctive label. Visit their museum at Tiptree in Essex to see just some of the remarkable, and unscrupulous, attempts to copy their style.

invokes images of a commercial endeavour, but Essex is home to the Wilkin and Sons **Tiptree jam factory**. If the word 'factory' conjures up industrialisation then that is wrong here because Tiptree jams are made from the fruit they grow, in the farm they own, on the land around where they make the jam. They are in the process of making the company into a trust in the ownership of the people who work there – that must be, as their jams are, perfection.

Right: As bright and shining as their jam jars, Wilkin's of Tiptree are very proud of the sign above their gate that was erected to commemorate a 100 years of jam making.

Visit the Jam Shop at Tiptree during early July and the air will smell strawberry sweet. Later in the year you might catch the scent of blackcurrants or even mulberries. Wilkin and Sons have been making fine preserves at Tiptree since 1885. Apple orchards stretch away from the car park beside the tea-room and museum where you can buy their distinctively labelled jars and see some of the machines that took them from pouring hot jam by hand during the last century to producing enough preserves today to service such special outlets as the Orient Express as well as shops around the world.

Tiptree's preserve some of Britain's oldest fruits such as mulberry and medlar. Their mulberry is exquisite with cream, on scones or pancakes, while the medlar jelly is traditionally served with lamb or mutton. It's also very good in the following fruit pie, based on an Elizabethan recipe, when the word for 'pie' was, unfortunately, 'coffyn'.

Above: Norfolk turkeys, roast , and cranberry sauce for Christmas and Thanksgiving, any way you like, all year round.

All recipes serve 4 unless otherwise stated

Medlars

Victorian gentlemen liked their medlars bletted (rotted in sawdust!) until they had acquired a unique, almost Christmas pudding taste, when they were served with a glass of port after dinner. Strange, but true, medlars treated like this are delicious, but also laxative, so it's probably safer to enjoy them in the following recipe that uses them fresh from the tree.

450g shortcrust pastry
Small jar good quality mincemeat
Jar medlar jelly
450g fresh medlars
1 tbs milk
1 tbs caster sugar

Roll the pastry out in an oblong, about 5mm thick, with the back of a knife gently mark it out in thirds lengthways. Wash and dry the medlars then, leaving the skin on them, chop as much flesh as you can away from the stony centre, spread two tablespoons of the medlar jelly down the centre third of the pastry, sprinkle the chopped medlars on top of this then spoon the mincemeat over the medlars. Fold one of the other thirds over the mincemeat then the last third on top of that.

Turn the whole pastry over onto a greased baking tray and tuck the short ends under firmly. With a pastry brush, paint the milk over the surface of the pastry and then sprinkle with the caster sugar. Take a sharp knife and make diagonal cuts into the top layer of the pastry through to the jelly. Bake in a preheated oven at gas mark 7/425F/220C for 25-30 minutes until crisp and golden. Serve warm with clotted cream.

The extreme tartness of the medlars adds a satisfying 'bite' to the sweetness of the mincemeat.

A quick way to enjoy medlars is to wash and dry them, score a thin line with a sharp knife under the flower end – as you would with a miniature baking apple, then put in a microwave for a few seconds. Watch closely! The stone-filled centres pop up. The instant they do, take the fruit out and carefully – they're hot – lift the core out. A small fruit shell remains that can be filled with a little medlar jelly and served as an accompaniment to lamb, or filled with sweet cream and served as a dessert.

Above: Lavender fields, rich with scent and the sound of bees. Increasingly used in cooking, a Victorian favourite, it's still the nicest of all smells for bedlinen, wrap a few dried heads in white tissue paper to put in a drawer or airing cupboard, or tuck sprigs into a small muslin bag.

If you're a cider vinegar fan – and if not, why not? it seems to help sore throats, can make your hair shine and adds serious style to a salad dressing – then you should try **Aspall's Perry vinegar.** Made only from fresh pears, it has an intriguingly oaky taste and a delicate scent of the fruit. Aspalls are the oldest family-owned cider-makers in the country. In the early 1700s a gentleman with the delightful name of Temple Chevallier came from Jersey to Suffolk where he bought Aspall Hall. A cider drinker at heart he planted apple trees and imported a stone trough and wheel to help him make his favourite drink. The cider trough is still at Aspall, in the original cider house. There is a lot of interesting history in the Aspall story including the fact that their orchards have been organic since 1947, but today's production methods are very much state of the art and they sell to Sainsbury's, Waitrose and many other retail and health outlets. Their sales and marketing director, Barry Chevallier Guild, suggests the following recipes for enjoying his product.:

All recipes serve 4 unless otherwise stated

Stilton pears

Try the subtle pear flavour of Aspall Perry Vinegar in this easy starter.

Halve, peel and core 4 large pears then thinly slice. Arrange in 4 small gratin dishes and drizzle 15ml (1 tbs) of Aspall Perry Vinegar over each. Crumble 100g (4oz) mature vegetarian Stilton into a small pan, add 75ml (5 tbs) double cream, then gently heat, stirring until smooth. Pour over the pears, then put under a medium grill for about 5 mins or until golden. Serve warm.

Perry pickled pork

Try Aspall Perry Vinegar in this barbecued pork recipe.

Mix 100ml (3.6fl oz) Aspall Perry Vinegar, 45ml (3tbs) olive oil, 60ml (4tbs) brown sugar, 15ml (1 tbs) paprika and 1 clove crushed garlic.

Place 4 pork loin steaks in a shallow dish, with a sliced red onion and 60 ml (4 tbs) chopped fresh coriander. Pour over vinegar, mix and marinate for 1 hour. Cook on a barbecue or grill for 10-15 minutes. Simmer marinade in a pan for 5 mins and serve with the pork.

Below: Crisp and salty samphire, grown here in its natural marshland habitat; its increasing popularity is leading to experiments in growing it hydroponically.

Opposite: Asparagus picked from Cambridgeshire, as welcome gift as a bunch of flowers.

If driving through the countryside is so relaxing that you need reviving then **The Silver Nutmeg** in Eye, Suffolk, is just the type of 'tea shop' to provide for your needs. *Here's their recipe:*

Carrot and walnut cake

300g grated carrot
50g sultanas
50g chopped walnuts
230g 81% S.R. flour or mix white and wholemeal flours
170g golden granulated sugar
110ml sunflower oil
2 medium eggs
Rind of 1/2 an orange
2 tsp mixed spice

Mix together grated carrot, sultanas, walnuts and sugar. Blend oil, eggs and rind. Add oil mix to carrot mix and blend together. Fold flour into wet mix, taking care that mix is not overbeaten as this will stop your cake from rising. Place into a 20cm/8inch deep tin, lined with greaseproof paper. Bake at gas mark 4/350F/180C for about an hour. Leave to cool for 20mins before turning out on a wire cooling rack.

Summer acres of golden wheat or winter fields touched with frost – whatever the time of year, the following sponge is perfect for 'showing-off' a locally milled flour. Light and moist it highlights the miller's art and the marmalade maker's craft – or vice-versa!

The miller's lightest orange sponge

275g wholemeal flour
50g cornflour
1 heaped tsp bicarbonate of soda
2 heaped tsp cream of tartar
275g granulated sugar
20ml vegetable oil
200ml water
1 medium orange
4 eggs
Tbs icing sugar
Jar of good, tangy marmalade

Line two 23cm sandwich tins with silicone paper. Sieve and mix all dry ingredients into a bowl, grate in rind of orange. Separate the eggs, add oil and water to the egg yolks and mix lightly. Stir egg mixture into dry ingredients, mix well, add orange juice, mix again. Beat egg whites until stiff, fold two tablespoons beaten white into the batter, add remainder of egg whites, fold in carefully, split mixture between two tins, bake in oven gas mark 7 for around 20 minutes, until just firm to the touch. Turn cakes onto wire rack, allow to cool. Assemble cake by spreading one layer with good,

tangy marmalade, top with second cake, sprinkle with sieved icing sugar.

Fresh herbs are available in growing abundance, and often found, as plants, at roadside stalls. The following recipe leaves the choice of herbs to you – and to the varieties you come across.

Below: The corn to the miller, the straw waits on the field.

Herb soup

Tear the bread into pieces and gently fry in the olive oil with the chopped garlic for a few minutes, add the water and wine, bring to the boil, and simmer for five minutes. Put into liquidizer, add herbs and whiz until the herbs are chopped and the soup smooth. Reheat until just under boiling, serve in hot bowls with more bread.

110g fresh herbs
2 thick slices bread
2 tbs olive oil
2 cloves garlic
1 glass white wine made up to 600ml with water

All recipes serve 4 unless otherwise stated

With a centuries-old tradition of market gardening, Anglia offers produce for crunchy salads, as well as winter vegetables.

Charred fennel and orange salad

One fat fennel bulb
Two big oranges
Drizzle light olive oil
Fresh mint to taste
Sea salt

Below: Cracked wheat, soak and cook in water until just tender then dress with chopped salad vegetables and a thick oil and vinegar dressing or cook for much longer until thick and smooth to make a dessert that can be flavoured with rose water or dried vine fruits and sugar.

Fennel is one of the crispest vegetables as well as one of the tastiest – as long as you like aniseed. Paired with cool orange segments it makes a wonderful accompaniment to cold meats or even a local brie type cheese.

Cut the fennel into four quarters, wash and drain it well. Drizzle with the oil, heat the grill. While the grill is getting hot, peel and segment the oranges, lay on a serving dish and sprinkle with torn mint leaves. Put the fennel under the grill and watch carefully as it singes, turn once or twice – the aim is to have a charred look over about one-third of its surface, but to keep the inside crisp. Cool the fennel, then lay it on the oranges, sprinkle with sea salt, and dress with a touch more olive oil.

Minted celery, cracked wheat and orange salad

Delicious on its own or as a bed for lamb cutlets, this salad makes the most of farm fresh celery, tangy mint jelly, and dairy yoghurt.

To 'cook' the cracked wheat simply cover with boiling water, let stand for 15 mins then drain, rinse under cold water and spread out on kitchen paper. Make the dressing by mixing the crushed garlic cloves into the mint jelly, then whisking in two-thirds of the lemon juice and finally the oil.

Stir the yoghurt well, then mix in the remaining lemon juice. With a serrated knife peel the skin and pith off the oranges then slice as thinly as possible without letting them break up. Wash, dry and cut the celery into half-inch pieces. Mix two-thirds of the dressing into the cracked wheat and celery, put it on a plate, top with the slices of orange, drizzle the remaining dressing over the top. Serve with chilled yoghurt.

Opposite: Charred fennel and orange salad

1 cup cracked wheat (burghul)
Half a head of English celery
2 tbs mint jelly
Half a cup of lemon juice
Quarter of a cup of olive oil
2 cloves crushed garlic
2 large oranges
Tub dairy yoghurt

Garlic potato roasts

1.3kg potatoes
2 cloves of garlic
Tbs olive oil
Tsp sea salt
Tbs chopped, fresh
herbs – parsley, coriander
or mint as you prefer.

Despite their rich flavour and chunky chip appearance these delicious potatoes are cooked in hardly any oil, and what there is, is olive oil so it's good for you anyway!

Scrub the potatoes well, remove any blemishes and discard any that have any green on them. Chop into generous wedges – a big potato will give 10-12 'chips'. Crush the garlic, mix it to a paste with a little of the salt, then stir in the oil. Having first dried the potatoes well, roll them well in the oil, put them on a flat baking tray, and then put them on a high shelf in an oven preheated to gas mark 7/425F/220C. Turn them over every 15 mins or so, they will take about 45 mins to cook to a crunchy brown crisp outside and a soft inside; sprinkle with the chopped herbs and remaining salt and serve on their own or with salad.

Beautiful Brussel sprouts

If the words 'Brussel sprouts' reminds you of school dinners then here's a way to bring their taste up to date.

Wash, trim and then quarter the sprouts, wash and chop the spring onions into 2.5cm pieces, peel and grate the ginger. Heat the nut oil in a frying pan or wok, toss in the ginger, fry for a few seconds, add the spring onions and sprouts, stir well over a good heat for under a minute, then squeeze over the orange juice, stir again briefly, sprinkle over rice wine vinegar and serve instantly.

175g Brussel sprouts
2 spring onions
Small chunk fresh ginger
Half a small orange
Tsp white rice wine
vinegar
Half a tsp of walnut oil

Right: Asparagus growing in the Fens, hand pickers use a slightly curved knife to cut just below the soil level.

Opposite: Oysters, padded with seaweed and tucked into a basket for safe transport. Neither the taste, or the packaging has changed for centuries. For a very modern way of eating the oysters try packing them into a pocket cut in a monkfish steak, wrapping the fish in young nettle leaves, gently steaming the parcel and serving it with a dressing of chilli oil and lime juice.

All recipes serve 4 unless
otherwise stated

middle

Derbyshire • Leicestershire • Lincolnshire • Northamptonshire • Nottinghamshire

england

Opposite: Celery in the Lincolnshire Fens – which stretch into Cambridgeshire and are one of the power-houses of vegetable farming in Britain.

Leicestershire is a land of rolling hills, of pretty churches, lush green fields and a forest called the National Forest that's the size of the Isle of Wight. And then there are the curries… from the prestigious Mem Saab restaurant in Leicester, or the friendly Sharmilee, both restaurants heaped with praise by locals and media alike. A visit to Leicester's Golden Mile, with its exquisite Saree shops, its tempting sweet Indian pastries, is a feast of food and for the senses.

Question: Where is Europe's largest covered market?
Answer: Paris? Amsterdam? Berlin?… hundreds of possibilities and then the real answer – Leicester, with over 400 stalls there's everything from the essential to the exotic, and it has to be one of the best places to buy Red Leicester cheese.

Say Melton Mowbray and think **pies**, succulent pork filled, hand raised, just right for a picnic in the beautiful countryside around the historic market town of Melton Mowbray or for munching on a walk alongside the Grantham Canal. If you visit **Dickinson and Morris** at Ye Old Pork Pie Shoppe in Melton Mowbray during the summer you can watch them making the pies – they even run 'make your own pork pie evenings' that over 20,000 groups from Gardening Clubs to Women's Institutes have participated in and enjoyed.

Raised pork pies, apparently, originated in Leicestershire. Centuries ago the wooden shape the pies were raised around was called a *coffyn*; today they are sometimes made in tins, long and narrow or decoratively oval, but some are still raised by hand in the traditional way, either around a mould or freehand.

Below: Ready for take-off? No! This snow white flock grazes on a hill. They walk down it, stately and calm, but need wing power to help them return their way back up.

Dickinson and Morris don't publish the recipe for their famous pies – it's a long kept secret, but the following recipe makes a classic 'raised pie' and when you've made this size that serves 4 a few times it's worth making a big one, perhaps in the sculpted, boat-shaped mould that looks so impressive on a buffet table.

Hot water crust

450g plain flour
Generous pinch of salt
110g lard (Tradition has it that some of the fat in a Melton Mowbray pie is butter, but this makes the pastry more difficult to handle.)
275ml hot water
1 egg

For the filling:
1.35kg spare rib pork – the meat should be in the proportion 2/3 lean to 1/3 fat.
1 tbs salt
Pepper
Pinch cayenne pepper
10g gelatine

An empty 900g jam jar or similar sized wooden pie mould lightly oiled on the outside or deep sided 305mm cake tin with removable bottom, oiled on the inside (the easiest to use is the cake tin).

Warm a large bowl, then sift the flour and salt into it, make a well in the middle of the flour, cover and keep warm. Meanwhile bring the lard to the boil in the water and stir until the fat is melted, then tip the mixture into the flour and stir well with a wooden spoon. Put on rubber gloves and while the pastry mix is still hot knead by hand until it becomes smooth and no longer cracks.

Working quickly – the pastry must be quite warm to use – take just over 3/4 of the pastry, keeping the remainder warm, and either form a thick, rough circle from the pastry, stand the jam jar or mould in the centre and pull/work the pastry up the side to required thickness – if using the jam jar turning it upside down helps. Tip mould sideways and roll gently to smooth the outside, make sure the top looks fairly level then put in cool place until set enough to gently ease out the mould. Or, if using a cake tin, divide the pastry into two pieces – one three times larger than the other – roll the large piece to a circle of between 1cm and .5cm deep, then lay it in the tin, patching any pieces that break.

Put the prepared filling into the pie, lightly roll remaining pastry to 1cm thick

and cut lid and any decorations – piles of simple pastry leaves look very good. Put the lid and decorations in place, then brush with beaten egg.

Have the pork trimmed and boned and the meat cut into small dice. Season the meat with salt, pepper and cayenne and chilli. Put the bones and any trimmings into a pan, season with salt and pepper, cover with water and simmer for 3 hours.

When the pastry case is ready, pack gently with the meat mixture – if there's too much, cook the excess in a covered terrine. Fix the lid, brush with egg and put into an oven preheated gas mark

Above: Melton Mowbray pie, the classic English picnic starts here.

6/400F/200C. Bake for 30 minutes then reduce the heat to gas mark 3/325F/170C and cook for a further 2 hours. If the pastry looks too brown cover with greaseproof paper. If the pie cracks down the outside wrap a triple thickness of greaseproof paper around and tie, top and bottom, with string. When pie is cooked remove from oven to cool. Strain the cooling stock, dissolve the gelatine in a little hot water, add to stock then pour carefully into the pie. If the pie has split, put it in a watertight container that fits the pie as closely as possible, or make a temporary bowl using several thicknesses of tinfoil, then pour in the jelly, chill well and finally trim away any excess jelly.

Right: Walnuts in high summer, a month or so before they're ready to gather and store, but just right for pickling if you can pierce a needle through the green casing and the shell inside. Once picked they're perfect with potted cheese.

$\mathbf{A}$ raised pie makes a wonderful presentation 'piece'. With practice the hot water crust pastry becomes straightforward, and with the purchase of a hinged pie mould a world of pies – pork, game, etc. awaits. Or you can visit Fortnum and Mason's glorious food hall in London and buy them ready made!

For a picnic, or summer lunch with a real taste of Middle England, try these two recipes, given by Dickinson and Morris of 'Olde Pie Shoppe' fame.

Potted Red Leicester & herb cheese

Place all ingredients in a bowl, set over a pan of gently simmering water and stir until melted and smooth. Pour into a clean, dry bowl or jar and refrigerate for 3-4 hours until set. Serve as an accompaniment to Dickinson and Morris pork pie

225g grated Red Leicester cheese
110g/4tbs thick double cream
3 tbs dry sherry
1 tbs fresh chopped parsley
1/4 tsp salt
Pinch white pepper
Pinch paprika

Lemonade

Wash and dry the lemons and peel thinly using a potato peeler. Squeeze the juice into a plastic container, cover and place in the refrigerator. Place the lemon peel and sugar into a large bowl and pour over boiling water. Stir briskly, cover and leave overnight in the refrigerator. Next day add the reserved lemon juice, strain into a jug, chill and serve.

8 large lemons
225g caster sugar
2 litres boiling water

Left: Rural idyll in Middle England, decorative fowl under an autumnal cider apple tree.

All recipes serve 4 unless otherwise stated

Opposite: Ostrich Steak Diane.

There's something very reassuring about a company telling you how it produces its product, and **The Ginger Pig's** pretty brochure does just that. As it explains, The Ginger Pig at Harwell Manor in Nottinghamshire derives its name from the coat of the Tamworth pig – see one, and the word 'ginger' is self apparent. It is a breed that used to be kept widely for its quality meat that produces fine bacon and ham. Slow maturing, it inevitably fell from favour commercially, but is now enjoying a revival with specialist meat producers who value its special taste and texture. The Ginger Pig's Tamworths are reared traditionally, piglets being born in straw-bedded barns, staying with their mothers until weaning at four weeks. There are no artificial growth promoters or antibiotics. The 'weaners' progress through a spell in a covered barn with open yard and finally to arks in the fields.

The farm shop at Harwell Manor sells their home-produced pork and pork products such as dry cured bacon – again their brochure tells you how they make it – and excellent sausages. They also sell beef from local, traditionally reared Lincoln Red cattle, organic chickens and local lamb.

Below: The ginger Tamworth, slowly recovering in numbers thanks to a Rare Breed Survival Trust initiative. An agile, inquisitive pig, if crossed with the slower, calmer Gloucester Old Spot produces 'Christmas Pudding pigs' with a real taste for adventure - and a considerable turn of speed.

*A recipe from **Oslinc,** 'The Home of the Lincolnshire Ostrich'. Here is a recipe for ostrich that uses the quick cooking of this meat to advantage.*

Ostrich steak diane

'This is a recipe the brave may wish to flambé in front of their guests'

Put the butter and garlic in a frying pan over a medium heat. Add the steaks, sealing them quickly on both sides, then cook for approx. 3 minutes on each side. While the meat is cooking pour the juice from the lemon and the Worcester sauce over the steaks, and continue to baste the meat well with the juices. Pour the warmed brandy over the steaks and ignite. Shake the pan until the flames die down, then remove the steaks from the pan to rest in a warm place. Add the Dijon mustard and the cream to the juices in the pan, warm through, then pour over the steaks and serve.

2 ostrich fillet steaks
1 tbs brandy or whisky (warmed)
85g butter
1 lemon
2 level tsp Worcester sauce
1 clove garlic
1 tsp Dijon mustard
112ml double cream
Serves 2

Left: Lincolnshire sausages, hand made to perfection deserve to be carefully cooked and served with lashing of buttery mashed potato and a good wholegrain mustard.

All recipes serve 4 unless otherwise stated

Opposite: The mighty Stilton, traditionally from Nottinghamshire, Leicestershire and Derbyshire, is only made in seven licenced dairies in these counties. This blue cheese with a unique place in British hearts - and on British plates - an unusual place to find it is crumbled over hot, oil dressed pasta, but it's quite delicious.

Celeriac is a versatile vegetable, known affectionately by some as 'The Ugly One'. **Jack Buck Growers** from Spalding, Lincs are so enthusiastic about its cooking and eating qualities that they have produced a leaflet full of recipes, from remoulade to rostis, showing off the 'strong clear flavour' of this 'phenomenally useful vegetable'. Best from November to April – like celery, it improves after the first frosts, it gives mashed potato a 'kick' and adds an extra dimension to shepherds pie, smoked salmon, fish cakes etc.

Winter Salad

1 medium sized celeriac
1 large red onion
1 large orange
Small handful fresh mint
150ml dressing made
from 2/3 light olive oil
1/3 red wine vinegar
Generous pinch of salt
Freshly ground pepper
Grated orange rind (see method)

Wash, dry and peel celeriac, cut into julienne, blanch for 2 minutes in boiling water, drain. Peel and slice red onion thinly. Grate rind from orange into dressing, peel orange with a knife, cutting away pith as well as skin, cut between segments to give pithless pieces. Combine celeriac, onion, orange and dressing, leave in fridge for 1 hour for flavours to combine.

To serve: add mint leaves torn into large pieces, mix salad lightly. Delicious after a game casserole for a warming supper or with hot bread and smoked cheese for lunch after a brisk walk.

The contents of the game casserole to go with the crunchy salad could well come from the same county. **Three Kings Deer** at Threekingham have a speciality farm shop where they sell venison from their own herd. Their venison sausages are made for them by Eric Phipps, a butcher at Mareham le Fen. Venison is naturally low in fat, as is meat from Soay sheep, and Three Kings Deer farm this increasingly popular rare breed. The Soay ewe is small and delicate looking, the ram has large sweeping back horns, both are very fleet of foot – as are the lambs, even when very

new, so farming them can be more like farming deer than conventional sheep. The farm shop also sells cheese from the Lincolnshire Poacher – Simon Jones at Ulceby – whose handmade cheeses are matured for 7-8 months, becoming strong and rich and perfect for a Poacher's Ploughman's.

Cheeseboard:

Mature Cheddar with fruit cake – a speciality cow's cheese from Long Clawson Dairy in Leicester. *Shropshire Blue* – a blue cow's cheese from Webster's Dairy, Leicestershire. *Poacher's Little Imp* – a speciality cow's cheese from Read and Sons of Alford, Lincolnshire.

Below: Try a wineglassful of Belvoir cordial, made in Lincolnshire, to disssolve the gelatine when making a chilled cheesecake - elderflower is a scented delight, the ginger a revelation.

All recipes serve 4 unless otherwise stated

heart
Herefordshire • Shropshire • Staffordshire • Warwickshire • Worcestershire
# of england

Opposite: Timeless England.

A recipe book written in 1985 by a resident of the rural Shropshire/Staffordshire borders contains such surprising delights as the ancient Roman, Apicius' thoughts on how to cook snails, flamingos and ostriches. The author of the aptly named *The Eccentric Cookbook* was the 7th Earl of Bradford whose family seat, Weston Park, lies in the Heart of England. A gourmet chef, his London restaurant, Porters in Henrietta Street, has been at the forefront of setting standards of excellence for English cuisine. Weston Park is one of the 'Great Shoots', a beautiful 13,500 acre estate with some 1500 acres of woodland and an abundance of wildlife.

Shropshire pie was a speciality in the 18th century, using some of the plentiful rabbits and pork fattened in the autumn woods. For special occasions, oysters and artichokes were added under the pastry.

Right: Matched pair? A splendid Hereford: prime example of its breed, and David Bellamy, environmentalist: ditto!

Shropshire pie

Cut the meat from the rabbits, chopping into neat chunks, cut the belly of pork into similar sized pieces. Mince the bacon and the liver from one of the rabbits, mix the two minced meats together with the thyme and form into small balls, seasoning with salt and pepper. Briefly fry forcemeat balls in hot oil until lightly coloured all over, drain and set aside. Arrange rabbit, pork and forcemeat balls in a deep 2.5 litre pie dish and tuck in pieces of apple and onion and the currants. If using artichokes, put these amongst the apple and onions; if using oysters, lay them on the top of the meat, just under the pastry. Pour the wine and stock into the dish. Roll the puff pastry out to cover the dish, cut leaves from pastry trimmings to garnish if required, then paint beaten egg over the surface, cut two slashes through the pastry to let the steam escape. Bake in oven preheated to gas mark 7/425F/220C for 15 minutes, then reduce heat to gas mark 4/350F/180C and bake until pie is golden and meat cooked through – about one to one and a half hours.

2 wild rabbits including livers
450g belly of pork
225g fat bacon
Dessertspoon fresh chopped thyme
1 tbs oil
2 dessert apples, cut into cubes
1 large onion cut into 1cm cubes
55g currants
75ml stock
Glass red wine
700g puff pastry
1 egg
6 fresh oysters if liked
4 artichoke bottoms, if liked, cut into quarters

All recipes serve 4 unless otherwise stated

Cider cake

For a shallow 13 x 20cm tin or two 18cm sponge tins
110g butter
110g granulated sugar
220g self raising flour
1tsp bicarbonate of soda
1/2 tsp of spice –
nutmeg or cinnamon or
ginger, or mixed spice
200ml cider

This traditional recipe is a speciality at the annual Hereford cider festival. It's also an all year round favourite and varies in taste according to the cider used and the amount of spice added.

Cream together the butter and sugar, add the eggs one at a time, beat until light and fluffy. Fold in half the dry sieved ingredients, stir in the cider and then fold in the remaining flour. Pour into the tins, that have been lined with silicone paper. Bake for 25 minutes for the sponge layers or 40 minutes for the oblong tin, or until a skewer inserted into the centre comes out cleanly in an oven preheated to gas mark 4/350F/180C. This cake is delicious served warm, or cold with cream, it also makes a good winter dessert with a drizzle of warm syrup or honey, or perhaps some gently stewed apples finished with a dash of the same cider as is in the cake.

Fern **Verrow Vegetables** come from St Margaret's in Herefordshire, tucked into the foothills of the Black Mountains. Their produce, from 25 varieties of lettuce, through globe artichokes to Greek Basil, is grown bio-dynamically, picked and packed to order and delivered to customers from Wales to London. They also sell direct at a scattering of markets, offering unusual produce, such as endives, and pepper grass, nasturtiums and borage flowers, all 'when in season'.

Tayberry ice cream? Or damson? Made with sheep's milk, **Shepherds Farmhouse** ice cream is flavoured with pure fruit, local wherever possible – except the mango! Juliet Noble makes the ice cream with milk from sheep that have grazed the sweet pastures under the Black Mountains. She brings out

Opposite: Shropshire Pie.

the misleading richness of the milk by using raw cane sugar – misleading in the nicest possible way, because despite tasting like 'the real ice cream you could buy twenty years ago' to quote *House and Garden* magazine, it isn't made with cream and eggs, but with 'whole' milk and so contains less than 7% fat. Juliet's partner Martin used to milk the ewes that provide the milk, but that's now done by a neighbour and he is involved in creating and running Food Fests where 'the many diverse aspects of food are celebrated in one event'. Their combined interests in food are reflected in the high quality of their product. To enjoy it, you must visit shops in the Herefordshire, Worcester or Powys area, or keep an eye out for their distinctive stand at shows and events.

Above: The pepperpot seed heads of poppies make a sculptural addition to the English cottage garden. Edible poppy seeds sprinkled over a salad of sliced oranges and thickly grated carrots make a similarly welcome contrast.

All recipes serve 4 unless otherwise stated

Roast ham with Shrewsbury sauce

1.4kg gammon ham joint
1 onion, whole
1 carrot, sliced
3 tbs golden syrup
3 tbs Demerara sugar
8 cloves

For the sauce:
2 tbs red currant jelly
1 tbs Worcester sauce
Juice 1/2 lemon
1 clove garlic crushed
600ml vegetable or chicken stock
600ml tsp thyme

This recipe is from Ercall Catering who serve it in the Club Room Restaurant at Blists Hill Victorian Town Museum in Madely, Shropshire, which is a World Heritage site. They provide all the catering for Ironbridge Gorge Museums.

Place gammon in clear water and bring to the boil with the cloves and vegetables – boil for 20 mins per 450g and 20 mins extra. When slightly cooled remove skin and score in a diamond pattern. Melt the golden syrup and pour over the gammon then sprinkle with Demerara sugar and bake in a hot oven for 20 mins, or until golden brown.

Bring ingredients to boil and gently simmer until reduced by half. Serve Gammon sliced with the sauce covering together with roast parsnips, red cabbage and onion and baby new potatoes.

There is something timeless about a rose garden, the heady scents of Old English Roses, now brought back to many gardens in the 'new' old roses offered by several growers. Their soft colours seem to glow in the dusk of late July evening as swallows swoop overhead. As well as a revival in interest in the sumptuous scents of the rose, there is also a British revival of interest in the taste of them.

Rose petal preserve

Gently spread out the rose petals on a clean white napkin, or kitchen paper, discard any that are bruised and browning. Trim any white from the base of the petals, then rinse them carefully in cool water and drain. Put the petals and water in a pan and gently simmer until the petals are tender – how long depends on the variety of rose. Add 4 tablespoons of juice from the lemons, and 1 tablespoon of lime juice. Stir in the sugar, bring it back to the boil and boil until the preserve is thick and syrupy. Put into sterilised jars and seal. This is wonderful with a good dairy ice cream such as Shepherds mentioned earlier, for a really special occasion – a summer wedding perhaps – champagne glasses of champagne sorbet topped with rose petal preserve and a small square of edible gold leaf would be perfection.

500g of rose petals – bearing in mind that the aim in making this preserve is to capture as much of the scented flavour of the rose, select the petals you use with your nose! Also remember that you don't want to eat insecticide – unsprayed roses are essential.
2 lemons
1 lime
500g of white granulated sugar
Scant 600ml water

Above: Past the edible stage, now drying to decorate the kitchen for the winter, the Cardoon has a place in every garden.

Butterfly lamb chops

8 butterfly lamb chops
Generous tbs red currant jelly
Tbs cider vinegar
2 sprigs fresh rosemary
Tbs chopped fresh mint

Opposite, left: Once seen only on remote Scottish islands, the Soay can now be found all over Great Britain, as here at the Heart of England. It is one of the few breeds of sheep whose wool can be sold privately and not through the Wool Marketing Board. Perhaps that's because much of their fleece is shed on hedges as opposed to waiting to be shorn.

This is an excellent dish for Sunday lunch, having marinated in the 'fridge all Saturday night, the chops simply have to be grilled and then served with new potatoes and a mixed salad, perhaps of mixed leaves with a good handful of rocket. All the ingredients used are the kind of good things stocked by many regional farm shops, good quality vinegar, fresh herbs, and redcurrant jelly without any additives, and of course succulent, local lamb chops. Butterfly lamb chops are a pair of chops not quite divided in two and flattened out, Valentine chops are the same but with the bone removed.

Melt the jelly over a low heat, mix with the vinegar and herbs, pour over the chops, cover and refrigerate overnight. Put under a preheated grill, cook for about 4 minutes on each side, basting with the marinade, allow to stand for a few minutes on a heated dish and then serve.

The Michaelmas goose

Goose is increasingly served at Christmas, but it used to be a great tradition at Michaelmas, the September quarter day, when it often formed part of the rent paid to a landlord. There is a growing number of farmers rearing geese for the table and the sight of a great white flock of birds wandering the fields is very special. Boiling a goose is an old fashioned way of cooking it, over the fire in a cauldron, but it also suits modern tastes as the fat rises to the top of the pan and can be taken off, leaving the deliciously tender meat.

Wash and dry the goose, put into a pan large enough so that it can be completely covered with water – a jam making pan will do, if you're desperate you can always joint the goose. Put the onion and herbs in the pan and cover the bird with water. Cover the pan – with foil if necessary, and then bring slowly to a simmer. The cooking time depends very much on the age of the goose. A young bird, that will have pale, flexible feet, can cook in 3 hours but a really old bird, with dark orange feet, can take 6 hrs or longer. As the secret of this recipe is to leave it overnight in a cold place once cooked so that the fat will partially solidify, it's best to start when you have enough time to see the cooking through to the end, however tough a bird it is. In any case, when the fat has risen take it off carefully and put it in the fridge, used to make shortcrust pastry it makes the very shortest, crumbliest pastry ever. If you want to use it to make mince-pies or other sweet dish, leave the onion and sage out of the recipe. The goose itself can be served, drained and cold, glazed over with a little honey mixed with wholegrain mustard or sprinkled thickly

1 goose – 5kg is a good weight for a goose, they come bigger and smaller, but bigger is sometimes fattier and smaller, bonier.

1 onion studded with cloves
Strip of lemon peel
Small bunch of fresh sage

Left: Organic celery, grown without blanching, to add a strong taste to soups and casseroles. It's especially good chopped in small pieces and cooked with haricot beans, some slivers of orange peel, cracked coriander seeds and tinned tomatoes. Perfect with the Michaelmas goose.

All recipes serve 4 unless otherwise stated

with grated lemon rind and chopped fresh herbs. Or take the meat from the bones and serve it in a brown sauce or with onion gravy or cold with pickles. Goose is certainly adaptable, a few pieces in a cassoulet of haricot beans and bacon is serious winter fare. And if it is a serious winter, try smearing a thin film of goose grease on your chest to cure a cough, or a little on chapped hands, meanwhile use a wing feather as a quill to write with and the downy feathers to stuff pillows. The thought of all that 'usability' can make you look differently at a goose.

Above: Heads of organic garlic, freshly dug, waiting to be taken to the farm shop. Roasted whole, they lose much of their pungency and add add a satisfying extra dimension to baked white fish, or tuck them inside a goose to roast.

All recipes serve 4 unless otherwise stated

Sticky plum hob pudding

A cross between a pudding and a scone this can be served warm from the pan or cold at teatime.

450g fresh plums
225g organic sugar
175g butter or substitute
225g wholewheat flour
1 1/2 rounded tsp baking powder
275ml milk

Wash, dry and stone the plums. Use 50g of the butter to grease a thick based frying pan, sprinkle on 75g of the sugar, lay the plums on the sugar, in concentric rings if you feel stylish. Mix the baking powder into the flour, rub in the remaining butter then mix in enough milk to make a soft dough. Using well floured hands take the dough and lay it over the fruit – the easiest way to do this is to pick up the dough as a ball, lay it in the centre of the plums and then lightly push it out towards the edge of the pan. Put the frying pan over a low heat, cover with a lid or a large plate and then leave to cook for about half an hour, until a skewer put through the scone comes out clean. The heat that the scone is cooked over has to be quite low, and it helps to give the pan a gentle shake every now and then. Once you've made it with plums, it's nice to try with lots of other fruits – cranberries are particularly good. Put a serving dish on top of the pan and turn everything upside down to turn out the scone, serve with cream or crème fraiche.

Cheeseboard:

Old Worcester White – a modern British hard cow's cheese from Anstey's of Worcester. *Hereford Sage* – a speciality cow's cheese from Monkland Cheese Dairy in Herefordshire. *Ragstone* – a soft white goats cheese from Neal's Yard Creamery in Hereford.

Opposite: Tomatoes, fry them, poach them, stew them, roast them, dry them, eat raw, juice them...the list could go on and on, including eating them with sugar - strange but remarkably good.

yorkshire

Opposite: Yorkshire ale, enjoyed all over Britain.

The wonderful, sweeping moors of Yorkshire are an ideal place to work up an appetite for the fine fare of the largest county in England. Whether or not the toffees and fudges that now sell world-wide were first made as 'shivery bites' to ward off the fell winds, they are as much a part of the flavour of Yorkshire as the famous pudding.

For an example of how good these 'sweetmeats' can be, try John Farrah's Harrogate Toffee, still cooked as it was in 1840, in open copper kettles, stirred by hand. It is 'real' toffee, old fashioned and proud of it.

The sweet theme carries into plum breads and gingerbreads, Elizabeth Botham and Sons in Whitby have been baking them since 1865.

A county of **cheeses**, Fountain's Dairy in Lower Wensleydale claims to be Britain's premier producer of English county cheeses,

Right: Toffee and fudge making the old-fashioned way. Tender loving care - and a strong arm for stirring.

Unique to them are Fountain's Gold, made from creamy Channel Island milk, and the revived Coversdale cheese. More cheese is made in Richmond, North Yorkshire by the Swaledale Cheese Company, they make cheese from cow, sheep and goat milk and it's all made by hand, some is smoked, some flavoured with beer, some even with applemint. Still in North Yorkshire, at Hawes, there is the Wensleydale Creamery where they make traditional hand-crafted cheese and have a visitor centre and restaurant. The emphasis is on ewe's milk cheese here; most of the hand-made cheeses produced by Shepherd's Purse Speciality Cheeses in Thirsk are made with ewe's milk, although they do also produce a blue-veined cow's milk cheese.

Above: Small truckle cheeses from Shepherd's Purse, dipped in brightly coloured wax they make a designer addition to the cheeseboard.

Above: A tempting bottle of Black Sheep, displayed on a handsome Jacob sheep rug, waiting for a thirsty shepherd to pass?

Below: Game – traditionally on display outside butchers for the Christmas season.

Any Yorkshireman, or woman, will tell you that a good cheese demands a good **ale** and Yorkshire brewers, large and small, are dedicated to quality. A good start for a Yorkshire ale hunt is a visit to the Black Sheep Brewer in Ripon, or the Malton Brewery behind Suddaby's Crown Hotel where you can ask for a brewery trip, and even stay the night. Then there's the Cropton Brewery with traditional ales and bottle-conditioned beers; you can try their wares at the New Inn. Hand crafted cask ales including 'Old Leg Over Country Stile' are brewed by the Daleside Brewery in Harrogate – asking for their brews by name is a sure fire way to begin a conversation in a pub.

Having enjoyed a piece of toffee on the moors and found the cheese and ale, the search for **bread and biscuits** is amply rewarded. Thomas of York Ltd are craft bakers and have 22 shops in North Yorkshire, Davills Patisserie in Ripon is an independent master baker, baking a range of traditional breads and cakes.

If beer and cheese isn't to your taste then the famous Betty's Cafes can offer you a mouth watering temptation of **cream cakes** and fancies, all served in a style that brings the 1930s back to life. If you've no time to enjoy a leisurely tea then at least buy the region's own tea to take home – 'Yorkshire tea' and 'Yorkshire Gold', a hark back to the days when it was appreciated that a tea should be blended for the local quality of the water because the taste of tea, just like that of beer, is dependent on the particular water qualities of an area. Yorkshire with its great moorland catchment has delicious **water**. You can even take some home with you because the Yorkshire Hills Spring Water Co. on Scholes Moor, Holmforth is busily bottling it. While on the liquid theme, a visit to Yorkshire Country Wines Riverside Cellars in Harrogate is well worthwhile – their own made elderberry wine is a delicious partner to a rich meat dish, perhaps a casserole of venison, or even roast suckling pig with the meats provided by the Round Green Venison Company in Barnsley. Ice cream to round off the gastronomic tour? On a gloriously fine day a sheltered corner on the edge of the moors tucked into the lee of a dry stone wall and a delicious ice cream, perhaps some of Charlotte's Jersey ice cream produced in Whitley, or some of High Jervaulx Farm's premium **ice cream** and sorbets or visit Oakwoods in Bedale for ewe's milk ice cream that's made and sold on the farm. Frozen yoghurt is produced at Highland's Farm in Scarborough and sold throughout the county.

A pause in the search for goodies might be a visit to Yorkshire's 'leading' craft shop, Womersley Craft and Herbs, at Womersley Hall near Doncaster – and even here there is fine fare on offer because they grow herbs and make fragrant herb jellies and fruit vinegars.

Above: An individual cheese press, just the size for turning a gallon of cow's milk into a farmhouse cheese, add a small piece of your favourite medium/hard pressed cheese into the milk as you begin to make the curds for extra flavour.

Opposite: Natural juice and water from Holme: Healthy, natural fruit juices and bottled water, perfect summer thirst quenchers.

From the Dean Court Hotel, York

Malton wild boar with a crab apple glaze, Womersley Hall herbs and Theakston ale

2 wild boar fillets, each trimmed and cut into 6 pieces (giving 3 per portion)
2 finely chopped shallots
225g button mushrooms
10g snipped tarragon
10g rubbed thyme
Small bottle Theakstons ale
275ml veal stock
275ml double cream
Small jar crab apple jelly

For the sauce: Sweat off shallots and mushrooms. Add Theakstons ale and reduce by half. Add the stock and reduce by half again, and then add the cream and reduce by half for third time. Add herbs, salt and pepper. Simmer for 1 minute and leave to one side. Season the meat. Seal in a hot pan with a little oil for 2 minutes each side. Place a teaspoon of jelly on each collop and glaze under a hot grill. Add any juices to sauce.

To serve: spoon sauce onto plate and arrange collops in centre. Garnish with poached crab apples (poached in white wine and sugar until soft) if required. Serve with buttered red cabbage, roast parsnips and roast chateau potatoes.

Fillet of Scarboro' Woof with a smoked Ribblesdale rarebit, herb oil, and oven dried tomatoes

For the tomatoes: halve tomatoes. Sprinkle with salt and pepper. Put one slice of garlic onto each half. Drizzle with olive oil. Place onto greaseproof paper and put into oven on lowest setting for 10 hours.

Oil – blanch and refresh and drain herbs. Place in blender with warm olive oil and whiz for 4 minutes. Season to taste.

Rarebit – sweat shallots, add white wine vinegar and cream and reduce by half. Add cheese, mustard and chives and simmer for 1 minutes. Season with salt and pepper to taste. Leave to cool for 1 hour. Pan-fry fish in hot olive oil for 1 minute on each side. Drain off fat. Spread rarebit mix over the fish and glaze under hot grill.

To serve: on warm plates place tomatoes left of centre, place fish on/off tomatoes. Drizzle oil around fish and tomatoes. Serve with creamed potatoes and a crisp green salad.

175-225g fillets of Scarboro' Woof
275ml double cream
2 tsp English mustard
1 tsp chopped chives
110g smoked Ribblesdale
1 small chopped shallot
1 tsp white wine vinegar
Salt and pepper
Tomatoes:
4 plum tomatoes
Rock salt and black pepper
1 clove garlic
2 tsp olive oil
Herb oil:
20g each basil, chervil, flat leaf parsley, and tarragon
275ml good quality olive oil

There used to be a lot of brewery coopers, because beer used to come in wooden barrels. Today, metal ones have become the 'norm' and there are only eight coopers working in British breweries. It makes the advent of a new cooper, at the end of a four year apprenticeship, something of an event and at Theakstons Brewery they celebrated recently by brewing a commemoration ale called Cooper's Butt. There was another, less public, celebration to mark the event that took place in the brewery yard, and followed

All recipes serve 4 unless otherwise stated

Opposite: Fillet of Scarboro' Woof with a smoked Ribbledale rarebit, herb oil, and oven dried tomatoes.

a 400-year-old tradition. 'Trussing-in' involves putting the new cooper into the beginnings of a barrel that is then completed around him. Spent yeast, hops, a little sawdust and some beer are added to the strange brew that is then rolled around the yard by fellow coopers.

Beer seems to attract history – or vice-versa! In Otley, West Yorkshire, there is a plaque commemorating the fact that Cromwell's troops drunk the Black Bull inn dry when they were camped outside the town on the eve of the battle of Marston Moor in July 1644. Cromwell's Roundheads achieved a resounding success the next day, defeating the Cavaliers lead by the dynamic Prince Rupert who had just relieved York. Perhaps, if the ale at the inn had held out a little longer, and the Parliamentarians been less disciplined as a result, then maybe it would have changed the course of English history?

The soaring ruins of Whitby Abbey can be seen for miles along the coast. Follow them as a landmark and you come to arguably one of the most beautiful settings for a town in the British Isles, and also arguably one of the best fish and chip shops. The **Magpie Cafe** has attracted visitors from many parts of the world, which is only fitting since Captain James Cook set off from Whitby to discover the world; his statue surveys the harbour and his memory lingers in a well endowed museum. If climbing the 199 steps through the old town up to the church of St Mary beside the ruined abbey makes you shiver, then perhaps it's because you've read the novelist Bram Stoker and recognise the setting for some of the scenes in his *Dracula*. Whatever the reason, achieving the climb is a great appetite builder so it's back to the Magpie, or a visit to the fishmongers to buy the traditional Whitby delicacy of kippers to take home.

If you keep on playing the video of *Titanic* then it might be that you're after some old fashioned, opulent interior design – in which case you should drive on from Yorkshire and visit Alnwick in Northumberland. At first sight it might seem a tranquil town, dozing behind its ancient stone gate, a delightful place to live, but ask for directions to the White Swan you will be on your way to a lost world. Enter the inn's dining room and you are walking into the first-class smoking room of the *Olympic*, sister ship of the *Titanic*.

To force **rhubarb**, the season for which is December to April, you give it a little warmth and no light. In a domestic vegetable garden that might involve putting an elegant terracotta forcing pot over a plant *in situ*, packing the pot with dry straw, and waiting for a few sticks to grow. Commercially it's a completely different proposition – and remarkably regional. The 19 rhubarb grower members of the Leeds and District Market Gardeners Association are responsible for 90% of forced rhubarb production.

Above: Sardines, hot smoked over oakchips at Whitby, with slivers of red onion, fresh horseradish sauce and hot brown rolls make a tasty and unusual, 'ploughman's.'.

Opposite: Recipe for good beer making - take one apprentice, put him in a barrel, apply liberal quantities of Theakston's know-how - and ale - generous hops, and shake well.

The plants are grown outside for two to three years, then transplanted to long, low sheds where they grow in darkness – so sensitive is the process to light that picking is often still done in candlelight or, at the very most, an extremely low wattage light bulb is used. Forced rhubarb should not show even a trace of green and light is the crop's enemy. It is still a labour intensive harvest and the tradition of enjoying an out-of-season delicacy still echoed in its traditional method of production.

Rhubarb Reviver

450g forced rhubarb
165ml champagne
Large tub organic yoghurt
50-110g comb honey

If, despite the good intentions, the richness of Christmas fare has struck, here is a gentle, restorative recipe using delicately pink forced rhubarb with a little of the festive champagne.

Wash, trim and cut the rhubarb into 4cm chunks, put it, and the champagne in a small, lidded saucepan, bring gently to the boil, simmer for a few minutes until soft. Leave until cold. Layer first the yoghurt, then the rhubarb and finally a chunk of glistening comb honey in tall glasses. Chill, eat and feel revived.

Not strictly in a food sense, but one allied to food production, visitors to Harrogate and Leeds have been one, very valuable step ahead of London fashion for a while. If an ostrich skin 'Kelly' handbag is a must-have then the price in London's New Bond Street has been around £4000 for bags made with South African ostrich skin. An enterprising Yorkshire ostrich farmer has slashed the price, selling bags in three different styles through mail order and local department stores. He added the big birds to his more traditional farming livestock six years ago when he and his brother imported 50 eggs from Namibia. 25 hatched, and he now has 350 birds.

Womersley
FAMOUS FRUIT & HERB DELICACIES

FOOD LOVERS GUIDE — BEST CONDIMENTS — AWARD

STORE IN A COOL PLACE
BEST BEFORE - SEE BACK

These award winning natural products are a unique gourmet selection of food accompaniments handmade from fruit and herbs grown by ourselves. The range includes herb and fruit jellies, vinegars, dressings, chutneys and other exclusive delicacies.

APACHE CHILLI WITH GOLDEN RASPBERRY VINEGAR

Ingredients: Golden Raspberry, Sugar, Spirit Vinegar, Chillies.

This product was specifically created to give a surprise subtlety to a salad. Also good with poultry or to accompany poached white fish, salmon or sweetcorn. Extremely good with oysters or raw fish. Use with Thai salads and fruit salads.

Contents **300** ml nett
MADE IN ENGLAND

Womersley Crafts, Womersley, Nr. Doncaster DN6 9BH • Tel Pontefract: (01977) 620294 Fax 620200

Left: Apache chilli golden raspberry vinegar: The label says it all!

All recipes serve 4 unless otherwise stated

north west

Cheshire • Cumbria • Greater Manchester • Lancashire • Merseyside

Opposite: Sweet treats from the North West.

Toffee is a temptation and as well as being made in great quantities in Yorkshire, it is very popular all over the North West. It is very sweet and very hard confection, inevitably a threat to teeth but it is delicious, melting in the mouth with a creamy richness and, as they say, 'a little of what you fancy does you good'! And there are more delights to toffee than just sucking it.

Try melting a handful of toffees very slowly in a saucepan over a gentle heat, with a tablespoon of fresh orange juice, pour the resulting sticky, fruity sauce over a sponge pudding and serve with custard. Or why not put some toffees in a plastic bag, attack them with a hammer until there are lots of small pieces and stir the 'crunchies' into a good vanilla ice cream, or thick organic yoghurt.

Right: Quality cooking requires quality implements, if a carpenter is only as good as his tools, is a cook only as good as their saucepans?

There are lots of very good toffees for sale in Lancashire, perhaps they'll inspire you to make your own?

Everton Toffee: such a popular regional speciality that the Everton football team is nicknamed 'The Toffees'.

Different types of toffee are made with differing amounts of fat and a variety of sugars, this classic toffee has a relatively high fat content and is cooked to a high temperature, making it hard, yet melt in the mouth.

Classic toffee

Put the sugar in a heavy based pan over a low heat with the water, stir until the sugar is completely dissolved and there are no crystals left. Use a pastry brush with a little water to brush down any crystals clinging to the edge of the pan, or the handle of the spoon. Bring the sugar to the boil and add the cream of tartar, boil without stirring until 300F/150C. Take off the heat, pour into a greased tin, and mark out into individual pieces with a knife just before it sets.

450g granulated sugar
110g unsalted butter
150ml water
Pinch of cream of tartar
A sugar thermometer is required

COOKING ACCESSORIES · WOODWARE

Above: A reason to visit the local agricultural show? Antique tractor racing offers noise, excitement and technical challenges and builds up the appetite for a working visit to the Food Tent.

Grasmere shortcake:

Add the ground ginger and baking powder to the flour, rub in the butter, add the sugar, mix well and put the mixture into a shallow baking tin lined with non-stick paper. Press lightly and evenly then put into an oven preheated to gas mark 4/350F/180C and bake for 30 mins.

Meanwhile make filling: cream the butter until fluffy then work in the icing sugar and enough ginger syrup to make a spreading mixture. Mix in the finely chopped preserved ginger and set aside.

Take the cake from the oven, while still hot turn out onto a board and slice in half horizontally. Spread the filling over the bottom half of the still warm cake, replace the top, press together lightly. Use a sharp knife to cut into fingers. If liked sprinkle with extra icing sugar. As an alternative you can spread the top with melted chocolate – not as baked by the post mistress, but still very good!

110g butter
220g plain flour
110g moist brown sugar
1/4 tsp baking powder
1/2 tsp ground ginger
(the quality of spice greatly affects the taste of the finished shortbread; Australian ginger is particularly good)
Filling:
110g icing sugar
50g butter
50g preserved ginger
A little ginger syrup

Warming flavours are a tradition in the Lake District. I remember going into a tiny rural post office to buy stamps for a holiday postcard and being greeted by the tantalising scent of hot ginger. We came back, a little later, to buy the Grasmere shortbread that the post mistress was locally famous for baking – so famous that she generally sold out very quickly and we, as visitors, were very lucky to get some. It went perfectly with a cup of tea from a thermos, enjoyed sitting at the edge of a lake so still that it formed a perfect mirror for the plump white clouds whose shadows moved slowly over the hills around us.

Left: The handsome Manx Loughtan originated from the Isle of Man. The rams can have two or four spectacular horns, the word 'loughtan' describes their colour - a soft, warm russset. Cloth woven from this wool is so special that in the early 1900s there were instances of it being bequeathed in wills.

All recipes serve 4 unless otherwise stated

Right: If a large part of the enjoyment of a good meal comes from the anticipation of it, then the Glass House at Ambleside offers visual delights in abundance to ensure gastronomic satisfaction.

As well as delicious, traditional fare, the North West offers a lot of innovation and the following recipe – from a very innovative venue – is certainly 'state of the art'.

From Adrian Sankey at the Glass House, Ambleside, Cumbria with his P.S. 'This recipe is brilliant!' It is!

Saltimbocca of Mozzarella

200g Mozzarella
125g pack Woodalls cured ham
1 small bunch sage
4 oven or sun dried tomatoes
2 courgettes, preferably organic
500ml white wine vinegar
150g dark brown sugar
2 tsp pickling spice
Olive oil
Salad leaves

With Woodalls cured ham (local producer), local pickled courgettes and salad

Boil vinegar, sugar and pickling spice until reduced by half. Slice courgettes and add to pickle, simmer for 2-3 minutes. Remove from pickle and cool, when cool add a small amount of pickle to courgettes and some olive oil to form a dressing. Split the Mozzarella into 4 portions. Place a couple of sage leaves and a piece of dried tomato on each, grind over some black pepper and wrap in a slice of ham. Place in fridge. Meanwhile wash salad leaves and dress, place Mozzarella under hot grill for 2-3 minutes until ham crisps and cheese just starts to melt. To serve: Place a ring of courgettes in centre of plate, pile on the salad leaves and place Mozzarella in centre and serve.

The Glass House is a deliciously modern association of fresh, exciting food and art. You can watch highly talented glassmakers working with molten glass, buy their wares, and enjoy lunch, tea, or a beer, or even have your wedding celebrations in the Grade II listed mill. Their publicity 'blurb' says it all. 'Glass makers for hot glass, the glass house for cool food.'

Spiced Mutton

With the growth of interest in rare breeds, the Herdwick sheep seems set for a major revival. Beatrix Potter spent considerable time, and money, improving the strains of Herdwick in her day, whether inspired by their quaint white faces – very 'Potteresque' or the excellent quality of their mutton, is a debatable point.

1 leg of mutton –
Herdwick for preference, as, reputedly, Queen Elizabeth II agrees
Black pepper
2 tsp dried thyme
Good pinch of mace
Tbs fine oatmeal
275ml strong cider
1 large green cabbage

The day before you want to cook the mutton, trim as much surface fat as possible from the meat, put the fat in a deep dish in a moderate oven – gas mark 4/350F/180C and cook for about 1 hour, until there is plenty of clear liquid. Tip this into a bowl to cool, discarding any crusty bits. Meanwhile rub the mutton with half the thyme and a generous grind of black pepper, and marinade it in half of the cider overnight. Next day, drain and

All recipes serve 4 unless otherwise stated

Opposite: Farmed Deer, not quite as nervous as their wild cousins, are a magnificent sight. Farmed venison can be less gamey in flavour, but a marinade in thyme and juniper berries with a generous dash of brandy adds robustness.

dry the mutton, mix the remaining thyme with the mace and oatmeal, press the mixture onto the meat, spread all over with the chilled mutton dripping, grind black pepper over the fat then wrap well with large washed cabbage leaves and put into a deep baking dish. If the meat is a snug fit in the dish the leaves will stay in place, if not tie them around with string. Pour over the remaining cider. Cook in an oven at gas mark 5/275F/190C for 30 mins per pound, basting twice during cooking.

To serve, place the parcelled mutton on a hot serving dish, leave it to stand in a warm place for 20 minutes, then slice thickly and serve with rowan jelly and a thin gravy made with the liquid from the roasting dish after the fat has been skimmed off.

Puréed potatoes, or buttered noodles go very well with the mutton, as does a crunchy cabbage salad sprinkled with caraway seeds and dressed with cider vinegar and a light olive oil.

There are Gloucester Old Spot pigs and wild boar at Sillfield Farm in Cumbria. Peter Gott and his helpers turn the pigs into hams and sausages, the wild boar into steaks and pies. They also make Westmoreland Sweet Bird Pies – layers of game and poultry in a pastry crust. Alongside all that, they make their own Westmoreland cheese and smoke many of their products. You can find them at agricultural shows and game and craft fairs all over the country. Peter in a distinctive striped apron – and bowler hat! Country and town dwellers alike visiting Country shows buy Sillfield Farm Cumberland sausages to take home for breakfast, and perhaps a prepared rack of wild boar for dinner, and their game pies are perfect for a picnic in the carpark. Picnics at shows and horse trials are often meticulously planned affairs that cater for a multitude; some families are famous for their carpark hospitality, and it goes on from generation to generation, a very British entertainment, come rain or shine.

Right: From wrapping delicate morsels for fierce frying or gentle poaching, to providing the nationally satisfying sandwich, good bacon has long been a mainstay of British cooking.

Cheese and herb bake

250g grated cheese – a Lancashire is ideal
8 slices bread – wholemeal for extra flavour
50g butter
1 tsp wholegrain mustard
1 tbs chopped fresh herbs
2 free-range eggs
900ml milk
Salt and pepper

Extremely simple to prepare, and quite delicious, the flavours in this lunch or supper dish can vary tremendously with the variety of cheese, different herbs and even the type of bread.

Toast the bread on one side, butter the other side, spread with mustard, and cut off the crusts. Cut into fingers and place a first layer, toasted side down, in a greased oven dish. Sprinkle with grated cheese and herbs then repeat finishing with a layer of cheese. Beat the eggs well, whisk in the milk, season with salt and pepper and pour over the cheese and toast. Bake at gas mark 4/350F/180C for about 40 mins until golden and bubbling. A distinctly sophisticated bake is the result of using sundried tomato bread with white Stilton cheese, slivers of black olives tucked in the layers and fresh basil for the herbs.

Below: Carron Lodge Farmhouse cheese, fine fare to be served with equally fine oat cakes, or enjoyed in wafers over a warm salad of beetroot and potatoes lightly dressed with a chive infused cider vinegar.

At Sharrow Bay Hotel you can enjoy a very special Sticky Toffee Pudding – but they won't give you the recipe, because there are 'secret ingredients'. The following recipe is another of theirs, bursting with the flavour of Morecombe Bay shrimps – just right to start a memorable meal that finalés with… Sticky Toffee Pudding!

Sharrow Bay Hotel, Ullswater, Cumbria.

Francis Coulson's Morecombe Bay Shrimp Bouchée

Finely dice shallots and cucumber and sweat off in the butter until transparent. Add Morecombe Bay shrimps and cook through for 2 to 3 minutes. Bring together with double cream, lemon juice, and anchovy essence. Season to taste with salt, pepper, nutmeg and Worcester sauce. Serving suggestion: Spoon into freshly baked, warm vol au vent cases. Garnish with crisp watercress leaves.

2 shallots finely diced
1/4 small cucumber
20g butter
275ml double cream
2 tsp lemon juice
Worcestershire sauce – 3 dashes
Dash Anchovy essence
Pinch nutmeg
Salt and pepper
110-175g Morecombe Bay shrimps

Cheeseboard:

Lancashire with Apple and Cinnamon – a speicality cow's cheese from Carron Lodge in Preston. *Skiddow Damson* – a fresh goat's cheese from Thornby Moor Dairy in Cumbria. *Butler's Wenslydale* – from Butler's Farmhouse Cheese, Lancashire.

Opposite: Cheese and herb bake.

scotland

As any Scot will tell you, Scotland is a land of heroes with food fit for them.

Oats have long been synonymous with Scottish fare – a famous brand of porridge oats features a kilt on the packet, and is called – Scots!. The crisp oatcake that goes so well with cheese was once a staple part of the Scots diet. The **oatcake** is traditionally cooked on a griddle, a flat heavy iron sheet, seasoned with long use and looked after with the kind of care that is so much a part of Scottish baking. Other griddle favourites are **drop scones**, or Scotch pancakes: a milk, flour and egg batter dropped in spoonfuls on the hot griddle, turned when bubbles cover the surface, served with butter or jam. They are fresh tasting, a quick and filling tea. And it would have been butter or jam in my childhood. My Scottish aunts never adopted the habit of butter and jam. Whether it was canny Scots thrift, figure-conscious consider-ations or simply appreciating that fine butter needed no adornment was never made clear. Just the same as never having sugar on porridge, it was the way it was done.

Scottish shortbread is justifiably famous. Crisp, yet melting, perfect with a cup of tea - or something stronger – it's the ideal biscuit for posting, and was, and still is, sent by Scots to the far corners of the world as a delicious reminder of home for high days and holidays. It seems a bit of a shame to point out that it is also widely exported so the recipients could probably have bought it wherever they live.

Another cooking implement with a distinctly Scots flavour is the spurtle – a stick to stir **porridge**. The spurtle is ideally shaped to reach into the corners of the pan, where porridge is most likely to stick. Once this delicious cereal would have been eaten from a wooden bowl – to hold the heat – and with a horn spoon – so that you didn't burn your mouth on metal – and once it would have been flavoured only with salt. Today many add jam, honey or syrup, and the traditional milk is sometimes replaced with cream or even fromage frais. A bowl of porridge, with thick cream stirred in, then caramelised on top with a layer of brown sugar melted under a grill and finally topped with a dribble of whisky, makes a notable winter dinner party pudding.

Opposite: The timeless majesty of the Coulins, backdrop to villages and harbours built to service the fishing boats that harvest the sea.

Left: Perfect symmetry of horns, fashionably long fringe, this Highland cow poses to bring out her best points.

Much of Scottish cooking has French connections – in years gone by many Scots noblemen frequented the French court, there have been French-born queens of Scotland, and the most famous Scots Queen of all, Mary, lived in France for eleven years. Her upbringing, her taste and her accent, when she returned to her homeland at 17, were all French.

Above: Scottish beef, the words themselves conjure up quality and taste, the glorious scenery its raised in must contribute to its perfection.

The chop of succulent lowland **lamb** in an Edinburgh butcher's window may well be called a gigot chop, cut from the top end of the leg – French 'gigot'. Once the chop has been cooked to perfection, perhaps doused with whisky, flamed, and brought to table it will be displayed on an ashet – the platter named after 'assiette' in French. Perhaps it is the French influence that lingers today in the richness of many dishes, or it may simply be a requirement for comforting food on a 'raw', blustery day, but Scots cooking is based on good food principles – a healthy respect for the food itself, imagination in its presentation and a degree of respect in its consumption.

All recipes serve 4 unless otherwise stated

There has long been a tradition of Scots fare being sent south. **Arbroath smokies**, the succulent, hot smoked herrings, once enjoyed never forgotten, were regularly sent down to London by train. Today they're sold in supermarket cold counters all over the UK and still a special treat. Potted with a little butter and a touch of allspice, they make an excellent starter.

The first variety of game that comes to mind in Scotland is the grouse, but the first in Scots cooking must be **venison**. The famous painting of the mighty 'Monarch of the Glen' shows the stag in its full glory in the wild. Sportsmen wanting to stalk red deer have been responsible for the great increase in their numbers in the Highlands. There are now over 290,000 of them in Scotland and the meat that comes from the annual winter 'cull' to keep down numbers sometimes makes its way into local butchers. While wild venison is, to purists, the finest, farmed venison is more widely available and of excellent quality when well hung. Venison collops – slices of meat fried in a little oil and butter, finished with a spoonful of redcurrant, or better still rowan jelly and a little cream – is a sumptuous, yet simple dish. The rowan berry is a natural partner with venison. Its dry tartness is good with rich meats and they may well have shared the same habitat – when the glorious berries are gathered on moorland in the Trossachs, the sight of them flaming against a clear blue autumn sky is as inspiring as a glass of the local whisky.

Wild **salmon** in Scotland was once pickled and sent down to London as food for the poor. Today Scottish wild salmon is a serious luxury, at the top of any menu specialising in fine fish. The great popularity of British salmon and the technical and husbandry abilities of fish farmers mean that some 40,000 tonnes of salmon a year are sent to market.

A plump, middle cut of salmon, moistened with a scant glass of white wine, a few fronds

Below: Kippers, for breakfast or tea, jugged or grilled, or soaked in lemon juice, flaked and piled on watercress for an appetising starter.

Above: A fine piece of fresh salmon is a wonderful inspiration - it could be seared, or poached, or baked, or fried, perhaps stuffed with herbs and mushrooms or flaked, or pickled or...

of dill or tarragon tucked inside, then wrapped in tinfoil and baked until just cooked, is a succulent joy. Serve it hot, with minted tiny new potatoes or the wonderfully floury Scottish later season potatoes or cold with a mayonnaise flavoured with the same variety of herb that scented the fish... to drink? a glass of local wine, and later a whisky, a malt to savour.

The brown **trout** fished from a remote Highland loch, cooked to perfection in a small hotel where the view from the dining room window is of moor, and sky, and yet more sky – the purity of tastes like these are the essence of cooking in a land so rich with wild produce.

And after dinner? Scotch **whisky** on a cool evening, by a roaring fire, a fine crystal glass in hand, or on a hot summer's day, in a long frosted tumbler over mountains of ice, with water as sparkling as the stream that ran over the granite boulders, through the peat, to the distillery, where it flavoured the whisky…

Whisky is made by malting – sprouting and roasting – barley; for single malt whisky this barley is then mixed with water and fermented, finally distilled and then aged in wooden barrels. For grain whiskies the malted barley is mixed with more barley, other grains and then

the process continues much as before.

There is a lot of water involved in making whisky, and different distilleries have, naturally, different water, so the end product tastes different even without blending. The barrels that the spirit is aged in affects the drink as well – it may be Glenmorangie, aged in old Bourbon casks, or The Macallan, aged in casks that have been home to sherry. The different flavours require tasting, slowly, until a favourite is established, then a 'wee dram' is like an old friend, full of memories.

A traditional drink, 'marrying' oatmeal and whisky, is **Atholl Brose**. Subtle differences in flavour come from the brand of whisky, the choice of honey and many families have their favourite combinations for friends to enjoy.

You can get a feel of the magical mixture of tradition and science that go into the making of whisky (including a glimpse of a resident 'ghost') by visiting the Scotch Whisky Heritage Centre on the Royal Mile in Edinburgh, beside the castle. Or visit some - or all - of the distilleries that welcome visitors, there's a list at the end of the book. It's a wonderful reason to go touring a glorious country.

Below: Whisky stills, amber and shining as the liquid they produce.

All recipes serve 4 unless otherwise stated

Atholl Brose

75g medium oatmeal
225ml Still Spring water
50g heather honey
Bottle Scotch whisky

You could make the Atholl Brose in the bottle that contained the Scotch whisky – it just means you have to find something to do with a few glassfuls of the 'spirit of Scotland' – pour it over a fruitcake, add to several Christmas puddings, or share with a few friends? A large decanter, perhaps of Stuart crystal, would make the perfect container.

Add the cold water to the oatmeal until you have a smooth, thin paste, leave to stand for an hour or so in a cool place, then strain through cheesecloth saving the liquid, squeezing the cloth to leave the grain quite dry. Throw the oats away – or with Scottish thrift feed them to the hens! Mix the liquid with the honey, pour into your chosen vessel, fill to the top with whisky and seal. This delicious drink should be shaken before pouring; it's a traditional drink to offer at New Year.

Above: Blazing rowan berries against a cloudless sky. The rowan - or Mountain Ash- is a useful as well as beautiful tree, jelly made from these berries is the perfect accompaniment to fine Scottish game, and a branch is said to guard against witches.

Say 'haggis' to a Scot and, like the rest of the world, they will either love it or loathe it. Either way they will probably eat it at least once a year, on Jan 25th, Burns Night. The ceremonial arrival of the haggis, that swollen sheep's stomach stuffed with oatmeal and spices, minced heart, liver and lights, is accompanied by bagpipes, the haggis attacked by a sharp dagger and the tasty mixture served with neeps – swede mashed – and tatties – potatoes mashed. There is also poetry, Burns of course, and whisky.

Today's adventurous chefs are doing different things with haggis, such as haggis ravioli, a home-made ravioli filled with haggis mixture, poached in stock and finished with a cream sauce scented with malt whisky – it is a treat to look out for. When drinks party nibbles require inspiration the following recipe from Deirdre Livingston, of the British Tourist Authority's Millennium campaign, appeals to haggis fans and foes alike:

Deirdrie's delights

First, cook the haggis. When cooked, slice open, put the meat mixture into a bowl and keep warm. Second, steam the swede. When tender mash well, add a generous knob of butter and freshly ground black pepper. Keep warm. Bake the filo cups as directed on the packet. When baked, fill each cup with a spoonful of swede, top with a spoonful of haggis, just before serving dribble over a little Scotch whisky. To finish, serve to guests with whisky sours.

1 small swede
Butter and pepper
Pack frozen filo 'cups', cocktail size
1 haggis
Tot whisky

If the prospect of eating anything – however delicious – that was cooked in a sheep's stomach is too daunting, then remember many butchers use a plastic covering instead – and they're less temperamental to cook – or there's vegetarian haggis as made by

Opposite: Gravalax: almost too beautiful to eat - but not quite!

Macsween's of Edinburgh, arguably the best haggis makers in Scotland.

There is a glory and romance in Scottish cities. There is the calm elegance of Holyrood House in Edinburgh, with the unsurpassed backdrop of Arthur's Seat. Once, in a Holyrood House somewhat simpler than today's but still royal, and still beside the windswept crags, Mary Queen of Scots witnessed the murder of her favourite, Rizzio. The weather on the moors, like the past in Edinburgh, can be violent.

The border towns also had a dramatic past; now they are peaceful, often handsome towns where good food, like the following recipe, is expected..

Selkirk pudding

5 slices of Selkirk bannock

50g Scottish butter

Jar of Keiller's marmalade

Tot of whisky (small glassful)

275ml pint creamy milk

2 eggs

1 egg yolk

Tbs vanilla sugar

Butter a 1 pint pie dish, use the remaining butter to spread on the slices of Selkirk bannock, then spread them generously with marmalade. Cut the bannock slices in four and arrange them, overlapping, in the dish. Beat together the eggs, egg yolk and milk, add the Scotch whisky, and pour over the bread slices. Leave in a cool place for an hour. Sprinkle the vanilla sugar over the surface of the pudding before putting it in an oven preheated to gas mark 4/350F/180C. Bake for 30 minutes, or a little longer, until well browned and risen. Serve hot with cream or ice cream

All recipes serve 4 unless otherwise stated

Mackintosh memories, art nouveau, exist cheek by jowl with the modern vibrant, cosmopolitan life that now is Glasgow. Food shops and restaurants are using local produce and creating new, exciting dishes. They're changing old rules, pushing the boundaries of flavour. You have to take to the moors, to walk and build up an appetite, to go back and eat some more.

The **border coast of East Scotland** is speckled with ruined castles, a reminder of an age of strife when England was the enemy, France the friend.

Above: Just some of the fruits of the sea from Scotland.

At the bustling Eyemouth fish market you may be able to buy a local lobster, sweet tasting – many say the finest lobsters in the world come from this coast, at their best simply poached and served still warm with mayonnaise. On the shores of the Firth of Forth, past the ever immaculate golf links at Gullane, through the idyllic village of Dirlton with its cottage-lined green and excellent inn where I once ate the finest mussels I have ever tasted, to North Berwick. Look out to sea, and the Bass Rock looms, home to fulmars and puffins, just as it is in John Buchan's fiction. A fitting view for a picnic with Scottish cheese and fresh baked floury 'baps', hot from the baker, or on to Tanatallon Castle, its rose red ruins romantic in the lowering sun of a summer's evening. More fish at Dunbar, where the Earl of Bothwell brought Mary Queen of Scots in an ill-omened wooing. Follow the coast, and Cramond with its winding alleys and pretty cottages entices, or on to Leith with an international reputation for seafood. Musselborough, with more fine golf links and Loretto School, has a claim to fame in its ice cream parlour that has lured generations of Edinburgh dwellers to embark on a drive to enjoy the ice cream cornets liberally sprinkled with sarsaparilla, or an oyster wafer filled with marshmallow and chocolate dipped – Scots are renowned for their sweet tooth.

Robert Louis Stevenson's 'hero' David Balfour knew Queensferry well; he admired the sturdy stone and slate buildings like the Hawes Inn, where Sir Walter Scott once stayed, waiting for the ferry to cross the Forth. You don't need to take the ferry today, the bridge takes you over the water to Culross, recognisable from a number of historical films, or Dunfermline, birthplace of Andrew Carnegie. And everywhere are restaurants and inns, offering good Scots cooking using fresh local produce.

Scotland is a land of history, and many small towns have ruins to visit, old houses to admire and today, new foods to enjoy. You can go mackerel fishing from Leven, or drive on to Lower Largo to admire the statue of Alexander Selkirk, the real life inspiration for Robinson Crusoe.

The following recipes were given by Wendy Barrie, Chief Inspector for Taste of Scotland. A total food professional, Scotland is her home and passion, and she is, as she says, 'Lucky… to earn my living where the product of the scenery, culture, food and drink is synonymous with quality the world over.'

Right: Fly fishing, however the day's sport goes, is a great way to build up an appetite, a fact that Scotland's talented chefs are delighted to exploit.

All recipes serve 4 unless otherwise stated

Chargrilled skewers of aromatic lamb

If using wooden skewers, pre-soak to prevent charring. Pre-heat oven to gas mark 5/275F/190C. In a bowl season lamb, mushrooms, courgettes and shallots and toss in olive oil. Leave for 15 mins to absorb flavours. Take tops off tomatoes and de-seed. Using a teaspoon, fill with haggis and sprinkle with thyme. Replace tops. Prop up stuffed tomatoes in a greased ovenproof dish along with 2 tbs water and cover with tin foil. Bake at gas mark 4/350F/180C for 15-20 mins until thoroughly heated through and tomatoes soft. Meanwhile, thread lamb and vegetables onto skewers and preheat grillpan. Brush pan with a little of the oil and sprinkle with rosemary. Lay skewers on pan and sizzle for 10-15 minutes, until cooked. Set lamb skewers aside and keep warm. Deglaze pan with wine and pour off residues into small pan, straining liquid to remove rosemary stalks. Add jelly to saucepan, adjust seasoning to taste, heat thoroughly and finally whisk in butter prior to serving. Serve chargrilled lamb with stuffed tomatoes, fresh berries and chive mash.

450g Scottish lamb gigot, cubed
A few sprigs of fresh rosemary
8 shallots
100g wild mushrooms
2 medium courgettes, sliced
1/2 jar redcurrant or bramble jelly
150mls (1 medium glass) red wine
25g butter
175g cooked haggis
4 tomatoes
Freshly milled salt and pepper
A few sprigs of fresh thyme
30mls (1 tbs) olive oil
Brambles/redcurrants to garnish

Cornucopia of Scottish soft fruits with bramble coulis and vanilla custard

350g assorted soft fruits
(strawberries, raspberries, brambles, tayberries or blaeberries)

Approx. 250g rough puff pastry

Egg white to glaze

150mls double cream, lightly whipped

For coulis:

150g brambles and 25g caster sugar

For vanilla custard:

300mls single cream,

3 free range egg yolks

10g caster sugar

2 drops vanilla extract

10g cornflour

To garnish: **mint leaves**

Preheat oven to gas mark 7/425F/220C. Roll out pastry to approx 2mm thick and cut into long strips 2 cm wide. Dampen with water and wrap each strip carefully around each of 4 cream horn moulds in such a way that each strip overlaps half the other as it entwines the horn. Wash with egg white and dip in caster sugar. Allow to rest for 20 mins before baking until golden. Remove from moulds whilst still warm and lay aside to cool. In the meantime, make custard by blending egg yolks, sugar, vanilla and cornflour in a bowl with the balloon whisk. Return to pan and thicken over a very low heat as required, being careful not to boil mixture. For coulis, liquidise brambles with sugar and strain. To complete dish, pipe cooled horns with whipped cream, fill, and overflow, with fruits; spoon coulis and cooled custard onto plate, feathering and finish with a mint leaf

It was Wendy Barrie who suggested I asked the proprietors of the Albannach Hotel for recipes using local produce. I first made contact with them in high summer – their busiest season, when I gathered they 'didn't even have time to do their own washing'. Their passion for the quality of their local ingredients was tremendous – they hadn't put together the same menu for two days running during the last ten years. They cook what is wild, or organically grown; much of their menu is built around fish, the catch of the day that is brought to the hotel.

From the Albannach Restaurant (hotel), Lochinver, a quote from Colin Crak co-proprietor: The recipe '…uses creatures that we really feel privileged to have available to us, and therefore involves the use of every last bit of flavour from the splendid animals that our friends who fish here for a living can supply… I don't include a recipe for the meat (crayfish) itself as I feel that should be presented incredibly simply.'

Opposite: Chargrilled Skewers of aromatic lamb

Left: Black Cock displaying, only one of the Highlands. memorable sights.

All recipes serve 4 unless otherwise stated

Brown crab and crayfish bisque with pepper and chilli dressing

For the bisque:
Bodies legs and shells of
3 x 2lb brown crabs
Bodies legs and shell of
large crayfish to 4lb (9
lobsters would be suitable
substitutes or shells of 8lb
langoustines)
1.5-2 litres well
flavoured fish stock
Hefty sprig of tarragon
2oz unsalted butter
1/2 doz small vine
tomatoes with stalks
2 tsp tomato purée
good pinch cayenne
pepper
1/2 bottle dry white
wine
6 fl oz whisky (brandy
could substitute)]
1 large onion finely
chopped
2 stalks celery
2 leaves fresh bay
Lemon juice and double
cream to taste
Seasoning to taste

To make the bisque: Roughly chop up the crab and crayfish. In a large pan sauté the carrot, celery and onion for 5-10 minutes in the butter without browning. Add bay, then crab and crayfish bits, turn over for about 5 minutes in the butter, adding a bit more butter if required. Add whisky and cook for a few minutes to cook off alcohol. Add fish stock, wine, tarragon, purée, tomatoes. Make up the liquid with more fish stock if required to cover the shellfish. Simmer for about 45mins then allow to cool slightly before briefly processing in a food processor, then straining through a conical strainer. Finally strain through a muslin lined sieve to remove fine debris, then reduce by about 1/3 to 1/2 before adding cream, lemon juice and a pinch of cayenne to taste.

To make the red pepper and chilli dressing: Squeeze out the bread to remove as much water as possible. Put bread and all ingredients except oil into a processor and whiz until smooth. Then add oil to machine (while running) at a steady trickle until a thick paste is achieved.

To serve: Ladle bisque into warmed bowl and place about 1 tsp of dressing at centre. Serve immediately.

For the red pepper dressing:
1 slice of good home-
made bread – I use saffron
(slightly stale is best) soaked
in cold water
Whole red pepper
seeded and chopped
1/2 tsp tomato purée
2 cloves garlic peeled
3 tbs good olive oil
Juice 1/2 lemon
Dash brandy
Dash good red wine
vinegar
Whole fresh red chilli
seeded
1/2 tsp paprika
Serves 4-6

Right: Lobster creels, a still life waiting for an artist. Poached lobster, a still life waiting for an artist, or at the very least some mayonnaise.

Roast trouçon of Lochinver landed turbot on samphire with roast courgettes in a salsa verde and saffron potato cake

4 x 7oz pieces of turbot
cut from a fairly large fish
450g floury potatoes
(e.g. Maris Piper) peeled
and quartered
**Large pinch saffron
strands**
**4 large handfuls
samphire**
**4 small mixed yellow or
green courgettes or 2
large ones**
Breadcrumbs
**Flour, black pepper and
olive oil for the potato
cakes**
A beaten egg
**Unsalted butter for
searing**
**Salt and black pepper
for the fish**
For the salsa verde:
Small handful each of:
**De-stalked spinach,
mint, coriander, flat
parsley**
Juice of 1/2 lemon
1 dsp Dijon mustard
3 tbs olive oil
2 garlic cloves and salt

From Lesley Crosfield, co-proprietor, at the Albannach

Prepare everything but the fish, which is cooked fast and hot at the end. Steam the samphire for 3 minutes. Refresh and put aside. Boil the potatoes and saffron strands in slightly salted water until tender. Drain and mash the potatoes, retaining the boiling liquid. Reduce this to 2 tablespoons (thus the little salt) and add to the potatoes with black pepper and a little olive oil if too stiff to form into cakes. When cool enough to handle, form into small cakes using a 2 1/4" cutter. One per person is sufficient. Roll in flour, dip in beaten egg, then breadcrumbs. Set aside on grease-proof papered baking tray. Roast the courgettes whole on a baking tray drizzled with olive oil, at Gas mark 5/375F/190C for 20 minutes. They should be firm, still resisting a knife. Cut into finger sized pieces, set aside. Whiz all the salsa Verde ingredients except the oil. Add the oil while whizzing.

To finish the dish, set the oven to Gas mark 8/450F/230C. Fry the trouçons in a hot frying pan with a knob of unsalted butter, skin side down only, for 3-4 minutes. Sprinkle salt and black pepper on white flesh. Remove to warm, buttered baking tray and roast, skin side up, for 7 minutes. Meanwhile, re-heat the samphire and the courgettes – microwave is best. Mound the samphire onto 4 warmed plates, tip the salsa Verde over the courgettes, coating them well.

As soon as it is cooked, place the turbot on the samphire, lifting the skin off with a spatula. The skin will come away easily if it is cooked, thus allowing the confident, minimum cooking that shows off this beautiful fish so well. Arrange the courgettes with extra salsa poured over, and a potato cake.

At the Albannach, turbot is often served this way, though a straightforward hollandaise sauce might be included, and a local kale or chard cooked with garlic and cream might be used instead of samphire. The variations are endless but the technique is the same.

Above: Langoustines: buying them off the boat at Oban. Driving inland to the moors. Poaching them in crystal water from a mountain burn. A jar of good mayonnaise, a bottle of good white wine chilled in the bubbling water beside our picnic place. A memory for ever.

All recipes serve 4 unless otherwise stated

Opposite: The only glimpse you may get on a day's stalking, but the perfect photo.

The Gaelic name for the purple staining blaeberry is 'fraochain' – that which grows amongst the heather – the Gaelic word for water of life is 'usequevar', and that is where the word whisky comes from. Put the whisky, blaeberry and a secret ingredient known only to The Marquis of Huntly and his son, The Earl of Aboyne, together, and you have a single malt Scotch whisky liqueur named '**The Cock 'o the North**'.

From the Tweed to the Tay,
from Cape Wrath to the Forth,
There's none can compare with
the Cock 'o the North

The Marquis is Chief of the Gordon clan, and, as such, the 'Cock 'o the North' – a title created by Mary of Guise, the French born Scottish Queen Mother of Mary, Queen of Scots in 1550. He also holds the titles of Lord Glenlivet and Lord Strahavon, named after the two famous glens in the heart of Speyside's whisky country. According to legend, this is the drink that the Gordons used to make to sustain them in battle, or to welcome guests to their Highland homes. Whatever the reason for its invention, it is a smooth, rich drink, just right for a chill evening, or even poured over vanilla ice cream, perhaps with some Scottish raspberries.

Cheeseboard:

Isle of Mull Truckle - a modern British Hard Cheese. *Crottin* - a fresh goats cheese from Argyll. *Loch Arthur with Caraway* - a speciality cheese from Dumfries.

Left: This giant, bottle shaped balloon has been to agricultural shows all over Britain, follow it and try a taster, but be warned, it's so delicious you will probably end up buying a bottle.

All recipes serve 4 unless otherwise stated

northern ireland

Ulster's Lough Neagh is the largest lake in the British Isles, and there are miles and miles of white beaches swept by Atlantic waves, so it is not surprising that fish dishes are a major focus in this area's menus.

Away from the sea there are ruined castles dating from the 12th century, quiet roads, blue mountains and championship golf courses. The famous emerald green fields need a liberal application of rain, but there are friendly hostelries to shelter in and the bonus of gloriously clean, fresh air when the breeze clears the weather. You'll be told that the only traffic jams here are caused by sheep, but there are plenty of other kinds of jam, made in the traditional way, in open pans, including a delicious 'Black jam', using only dark fruits.

The quality of dairy produce reflects the lush grass and the tranquillity of the cows. If you come to fish the salmon, then many inns will cook your catch skilfully – and you can celebrate their art with a glass of Irish whiskey.

Opposite: Perhaps the glorious scenery affects the flavour of the meat, but certainly Ulster mutton is very good and deserves serving with some locally made sloe jelly.

The following recipes were given by Corinne McAlister, from The Morning Star in Pottinger's Entry, Belfast, who says "Some of our dishes are very traditional and others more exotic, but I have chosen some of the traditional, staple variety which would be used seasonally when the produce is at its best."

Pot of steaming Strangford mussels

Wash and scrub the mussels under cold running water and remove 'beards'. Do not use mussels that are already open or have cracked shells. Put butter in large saucepan and melt. Add finely chopped garlic. Cook gently for a few minutes. Add mussels, white wine, cream, salt and pepper. Cover saucepan with a lid. Cook for about 4 minutes, shaking pan occasionally, until all the mussels have opened. Place in serving dishes (we use a Pyrex pot with fitted lid) and serve immediately with crusty bread. The mussels are simply cooked and the cream and wine stock is delicious as a soup. Preparation time: 10 minutes. Cooking time: 8 minutes. Serves 3-4 as a main course, 6-8 as a starter

60 fresh mussels
1/4 bottle dry white wine
2 tbs butter
4 cloves garlic
Salt and pepper
2 tbs chopped parsley
275ml fresh cream

Below: Many years of grazing have helped form the landscape and careful husbandy has made for lush fields that feed the cows that graze the land and keep the landscape beautiful.

Nettle soup (early spring)

**3 cups fresh young
nettle leaves
75g butter
20g oatmeal or porridge
oats
600ml chicken or
vegetable stock
275ml pint milk
138ml pint cream**
Serves 6-8

Wear gloves while harvesting Nettles (and pick from an area that has not been polluted i.e. car exhaust from side of road) before 1st May otherwise they are very difficult to harvest and are too strong in flavour.

Chop nettle leaves or process. Melt butter in large saucepan. Mix in oatmeal and stir until golden. Remove pan from heat and add stock. Bring stock mix to boil and add milk. When mixture has boiled again, add chopped nettle leaves, season and cook for a few minutes. Remove mixture from heat, add a swirl of cream and serve. Serve with fresh wheaten bread or Guiness wheaten bread. For a very rich soup add a dash of Irish whiskey. Preparation time: 10 minutes (after you have gathered the nettles). Cooking time: 15 minutes.

The giant, Finn McCool, warrior of Ulster and Commander of the King of Ireland's armies, must have had a mighty appetite if, as the ancients believed, he built the Giant's Causeway in North Antrim. The explanation that this amazing landscape, more reminiscent of the moon than a beach, is a geological accident and made up of lava may appeal to your sense of logic, but on a blustery day, with the wind and the sea roaring you can almost hear the hammer blows of the mighty Finn.

If the sight of the Mountains of Mourne sweeping down to the sea stirs your appetite as well as your tears, then the Ham and Cabbage soup cooked and served at Grange Lodge Dungannon both satisfies hunger and soothes the senses.

Above: Spring - a time of plenty in the traditional farm yard.

Below: Placid waters, calm after the storm, a day's fishing then home to a hearty casserole of mixed fish and vegetables finished with a touch of whiskey.

**All recipes serve 4 unless
otherwise stated**

Opposite: Steaming Strangford mussels.

Recipe from Norah Brown MBE

Ham and cabbage soup

1 lean unsmoked ham
shank
1 can (440ml) Caffrey's
Irish Ale
2 tbs olive oil
50g butter
Sprigs of thyme, parsley
and bay leaf
2 finely chopped large
onions
2 crushed garlic cloves
3 ltrs cold water
700ml chicken stock
1 small finely shredded
Savoy cabbage with
plenty of green leaves
1 pkt fresh green soup
vegetables (chopped)
2 finely diced carrots
1/2 finely diced small
turnip
6 large peeled potatoes
roughly cut into 2.5cm
cubes
225g soup mix... pearl
barley etc.
Black pepper
75g cornflour blended in
125ml water
Serves 12-15

Soak ham in cold water for at least 12 hours, remove and rinse well. Put the shank in a large heavy-base saucepan, add the water, thyme, parsley, bay leaves and Caffrey's ale. Bring to the boil and simmer gently for 2-3 hours, until shank is tender and comes off the bone easily. Remove shank, strain stock into a large bowl and leave to cool overnight. Next day, skim off any surplus fat. Using the heavy-base saucepan melt the butter, add oil, onion, garlic and black pepper. Sauté over a gentle heat, stirring regularly until transparent, do not brown. Add carrot, turnip and potato, stir gently for about 5 mins, until well tossed with the onion mixture, now add the bacon and chicken stock together with the soup mix. Bring to the boil and simmer for 20-25 minutes, until the vegetables are almost cooked. Add the shredded cabbage and green soup vegetables, bring back to the boil and simmer for a further 20 minutes. Add finely shredded ham and the blended cornflour, stirring continuously. Bring back to the boil for 2-3 minutes until slightly thickened. Serve with toasted soda farl. This soup is best made the day before use to allow all the flavours to come together!

Potato bread

Makes 4 farls of 18 cakes with 3" (7 1/2cm) cutter.

500g peeled potatoes
130g plain flour
50g butter
1 tsp salt, pepper to
taste

Boil potatoes, peel and mash until very smooth and free from lumps. Add the salt, pepper and butter, then work in 125g of flour to make a pliable dough. With the remaining flour, turn onto a floured surface and roll into a circular shape about 6mm thick and 22cm in diameter using a little extra flour if necessary. Cut into 4 farls or circles with the cutter and bake for about 3-4 minutes on a lightly floured, pre-heated griddle or heavy based frypan until lightly browned on each side, cool. When required, fry in a little olive oil or bacon fat to serve. Perfect with Ulster Fry or grilled steak – a great base for scrambled eggs with smoked salmon, or with sautéed mushrooms, or grilled tomato. Great for the kids to cut into animal shapes and served with beans. Will also freeze well.

Below: Ulster pigs provide wonderful hams and bacon. An old - and environ-mentally friendly so very modern - way to cook a large ham is to start off by boiling it for half an hour then finish it in a hay box. Make one by taking a heavyweight cardboard box, lining it with hay or other insulating material, inside that make a waterproof cocoon out of aluminium foil, pop in the pan containing the hot ham and cooking liquid. Cover with more hay. Leave overnight.

Below: Bushmills distillery

The Charr is a non-migratory, lake dwelling fish belonging to the salmon family. It usually grows to between 26 and 30cm in length, although 40cm specimens are not uncommon. These fish like deep water, and although the Windermere Charr is so well known that it has its own recipe for potting, those to be fished in Ulster during the peak months of May and June provide just as much sport for the dedicated angler, and just as good fish for the following recipe.

Potted Charr

Gut, wash and dry the fish, sprinkle with salt, lay on a drainer, or thick pad of kitchen paper, and leave overnight in the refrigerator. Meanwhile clarify the butter by melting it gently then straining into a bowl and leaving until set. In the morning take off the hard, clarified butter and throw away remaining liquid. When ready to pot the fish, take them out of the refrigerator, remove and discard their heads, wipe the remainder well and pat dry, then put into a deep dish lined with silicone paper. Melt the clarified butter, stir the seasonings into it and pour over the fish, then bake the pot for two hours in a slow oven. When cooked, put to cool. Then refrigerate. Carefully remove the potted char from mould and place onto a serving dish, offer with hot toast.

Charr, as many as you have. The following quantities of seasoning and butter are for 2 fish

1 tbs salt
1/4 tsp white pepper
Good pinch cayenne pepper
Good pinch ground cloves
Small pinch mace
450g butter

Cheeseboard:

Ballyblue – a blue cow's cheese from Fivemiletown Creamery in C. Tyrone.

Bushmills porridge

1 cup (100g) white speedicook oat flakes
3 cups 500ml cold water
1 tsp salt
Demerara sugar to taste
Fresh cream
4 tbs Bushmills whiskey

Put all the oatflakes water and salt in a cast iron pot with lid, stir well and place in bottom left hand oven of a four oven Aga cooker overnight. Alternatively, place in covered saucepan, bring to boiling point and simmer for 10-15 minutes. To serve: Divide into 4 cereal bowls, sprinkle with brown sugar to taste, pour the malt whiskey around the edge, easing with a spoon until the porridge almost floats. Add fresh cream according to taste.

Right: Fresh shellfish that smells of the clear coastal waters requires only the simplest of cooking and serving with a homemade mayonnaise, or in the case of scallops, frying quickly alongside some bacon for breakfast.

Above: Fresh fish is bright of eye, smells of the sea, and shines like this pair of mackerel destined for the barbeque.

All recipes serve 4 unless otherwise stated

countrywide

Cheesemaking has gone on continuously in Britain since early man first discovered that curdled milk lasted longer than fresh, and that if it was then drained it was far easier to carry. The supposition is that the rennet naturally present in the animal stomach bags the early nomads carried their milk in would turn the milk to curds. Today many cheesemakers still use animal rennet, but there is a growth in the use of the vegetarian rennet that suits all consumers. The tradition of farmhouse cheeses, made by the farmer's wife and milkmaids and sold at local markets sounds today like a rural idyll – as long as you forget the hard work it entailed, but cheese is still being made by time honoured methods, and that graded by the Milk Marketing Board under a scheme set up in 1954 is still made 'on the farm'.

The great growth in the varieties of cheese being made in Britain today means that the putting together of a cheeseboard can be a geographical adventure: red cheese from Leicester, Blue cheese from Oxford, the classic yellow Cheddar, originally and still made in Somerset but also from one end of Britain to the other. There are artisan cheesemakers producing over 130 different cheeses and speciality cheese makers who combine fine cheese and crystallised ginger, pickle, or nuts.

Opposite: Fields of gold and purple: a sea of wheat, gently blown into waves and currents, splashed by rain, and warmed by the sun, set off by lavender.

Cooking with British cheese has never been more exciting and the recipe on the next page will taste uniquely different depending on the varieties you choose.

Below: The ultimate farmhouse kitchen with all the fine fare imaginable, just waiting for a housefull of hungry guests.

Three Counties cheese terrine

165g of each of three varieties of British cheese, e.g. Cheshire, Oxford Blue and Red Leicester, or goats' milk cheddar, soft goats' cheese with chives and smoked ewe's cheese.

75g of chopped apples – again the variety of apple affects the flavour of the dish - soaked in lemon juice. Try Russet apples with Wensleydale, or Cox's with Cheddar

75g chopped celery or grated celeriac

Optional 50g chopped nuts

Line a long, narrow tin with silicone paper. Prepare cheese according to type, the harder, matured cheeses are best cut into thick slices, varieties such as Wensleydale should be crumbled, soft cheeses should be carefully cut into thick pieces. Prepare the fruit and vegetables. Layer one cheese in the bottom of the tin, cover with chopped apple, layer with the second cheese, layer with celery, finish with the final cheese, press down lightly. Refrigerate for at least an hour. Turn out carefully on a serving dish lined with salad leaves, serve with hot breads and pickle.

You wouldn't be surprised to find Jordans Cereals being sold direct at a farmer's market, the produce of a farmer with an enterprising approach to healthy eating. Their fresh, country-style packaging and natural taste could easily have come direct from the farm, but Jordan's are big business.

They are a company with a history, having begun milling grain in 1855 they built their current mill – Holme Mill, at Biggleswade in Bedfordshire, in 1896. Today they buy 20,000 tonnes of Conservation Grade grain a year and that's more than the total UK output of organic grain. They are the only muesli manufacturer to mill their own oats, with a host of 'firsts' to their credit – first 'no artificial ingredients, in 1973, first cereal bar in 1973, first cereal to contain whole raspberries – 1995'. They have a record of producing original, market leading products – and what they make is delicious for children and adults alike – a fact that isn't always true of 'health' products. Their Original Crunchy, a toasted oat cereal with honey, almonds and raisins, was launched in 1980, at the same time as Bill Jordan was becoming involved in the development of the Guild of Conservation Grade Producers and the Conservation Grade Standard. By definition, the Conservation Grade Standard covers many of the 'best aspects of organic farming without organic farming's current problems of volume and sustainability'.

The aim of the Guild, in their own words is 'to promote the concept of Conservation Grade food in the mutual interests of consumers, the environment and all those involved in food production and distribution.' There are high standards set for participating growers, combining traditional farming methods such as crop rotation for soil fertility and selected modern farming methods with strict controls on the use of chemicals such as pesticides and herbicides to ensure there are no adverse effects on soil and organic matter and no permanent residue left in the soil. So that all standards can be strictly monitored, all product is traceable to individual growers in the scheme.

Below: One of the earliest factors in civilisation, the ability to grow good grain, is as important today as it ever was, and the farmer as justifiably proud of his art.

Right: Wine is produced all over Britain. This one, from Penshurst in Kent is made from grapes grown on the beautiful banks of the fertile Medway Valley. Crisp and delicious, it's perfect with a host of foods, or just on its own as the sun slips over the Wealden horizon.

Milk and cream have provided British desserts for as long as there have been recorded recipes, and no doubt, earlier. Syllabub, tradition has it, was initially formed by milking a cow straight into a container of wine or cider, the resulting mix of milk and curdling agent resulting in a bubbly curd that could be spooned into glasses. Not many modern kitchens have room for a cow, so the following recipe gives an idea of the taste of the original without the upheaval.

Syllabub

Stir the honey into the white wine, mix in the juice of half the lemon, and a few thin strands of lemon rind. Whisk the egg whites until they make stiff peaks, fold in the sugar, then fold in the wine mixture. Whisk the cream until it is thick, but not dry, then fold it into the egg white mixture. Carefully spoon the syllabub into serving glasses – long slim ones are best, leave for 6 to 12 hours in a cool place – it will separate into two layers. Serve sprinkled with crystallised flower petals, and traditionally, ratafia biscuits. Untraditionally it's fun to serve the syllabub with a straw through the cream top to the alcoholic bottom.

275ml double cream
110g castor sugar
1 lemon
138ml white wine
Dessertspoon runny honey
2 egg whites

Another recipe to make the most of fine quality fresh milk:

Baked custard

Either take a thin strip of orange peel, or rub 5 or 6 sugar cubes over the surface of the orange, if using the strip, add it and the castor sugar to the milk in a small boiling pan, or add the orange flavoured cubes to the milk. Heat gently to just below boiling, set aside. Break two of the whole eggs into a bowl, separate the remaining eggs, add the yolks to the bowl

600ml fresh milk
10g unsalted butter
4 eggs
1 tbs castor sugar or several sugar cubes (see method)
1 orange
Nutmeg if liked

Jordans also source organic produce for their Organic Muesli and Organic Crunchy and are actively involved in furthering the sustainability of commercial organic farming.

Milk is still being delivered to doorsteps in Britain. As well as the 'biggies' such as Unigate there are hundreds of farmers milking, pasteurising and bottling on the farm, then delivering direct to local families who enjoy not only the quality of the milk, but often also walking in the fields the cows graze. In a new initiative, goats' milk is being brought to the consumer by doorstep deliveries in some areas, Unigate are using the South East goats' milk producer, Brownings of Cowden, to provide the milk they are offering for home delivery. Supermarkets sell vast quantities of milk – cows, goats and non animal products such as soya. To find sheep's milk usually requires a little more effort, but sometimes it is to be found on sale, by the glass, at agricultural shows and fairs. The occasional outlet even offers British buffalo milk!

All recipes serve 4 unless otherwise stated

Opposite: Syllabub.

and keep the whites for another dish. Mix the eggs well, but do not beat, the mixture should be smooth, not frothy. When the milk is cool pour it into the eggs, mix well, then strain into a 900ml pie or soufflé dish that has been greased with half the butter. If using nutmeg sprinkle a little over the surface of the custard, drop the remaining butter in tiny pieces onto the surface, put the dish into a baking dish containing 2.5mm of water, bake at gas mark 4/350F/180C for 35 minutes, until set and golden on top.

This delicately delicious dish can also be baked in small individual ramekins, or custard cups. The flavour of the milk can be varied, by using different citrus peels, or soaking a few scented rose petals in the milk before heating, or using a vanilla pod, or some cardamom – the inspiration is yours.

Above: The bantam cock has a crow as loud as any of his larger cousins, whilst his hens' eggs although small are especially delicious. Farm shops countrywide offer a choice of eggs from quail through hens to goose.

If the national dish of Britain is the curry, then the national take away must be the sandwich. The 1980s lunchtime queues for Marks and Spencers Prawn Sandwiches are things of legend. The 'yuppie' generation's working lunch revolved around the juicy prawns, the iceberg lettuce and oozing mayonnaise.

'Prêt à Manger' gave a recipe for the Millennium chapter, for what they saw as a perfect future sandwich – fast to make, depending for its impact on impeccable quality and freshness, simple to eat yet satisfying and delicious. As a company, this leading sandwich provider makes just what their customers want – at speed. Creating a 'steak and chips' sandwich using beef from the Specially Selected brand promoted by the Scotch Quality Beef and Lamb Association is an example. It is so successful that the company now buys the beef at the rate of 1 ton a week; their sandwich description

Above: 'The best thing since sliced bread' is an out of date remark now that there is so much tasty, crusty bread on offer. From local baker to supermarket, the choice of breads has risen almost as quickly as a good, wholemeal loaf. Try a grainy wholemeal with regional cheese and a mature chutney or crunchy pickle like those made by Darenth Valley Pickling Company, one of the fine preserve makers in Britain.

All recipes serve 4 unless otherwise stated

explains why: rare topside of Specially Selected Scotch Beef on granary bread and served with roasted tomatoes, mixed lettuce, horseradish mayonnaise and Pret a Manger's own brand crisps. Sounds good!

Todd's Vintry on the famous **Pantiles** in Tunbridge Wells, Kent, is an excellent example of the fine retail shops that sell regional specialities amongst imported delights and countrywide favourites. There is biltong, produced by a South African living and working in London, hanging above a chill counter full of a great range of cheeses from home and abroad – with a strong emphasis on French cheese, because the owner, Michel, is French, and he proclaims his partialities on a blackboard in the shop: "If it isn't French it isn't fromage"!

There are tins of Dorset biscuits, jars of conserves from all over the country, and local farmhouse fudge alongside handmade truffles. The crowded shelves are full of shining jars and pretty packages and the smell as you step off the historic paved walkway is subtly spicy and welcoming, as are the dozens of bottles of fine wines.

Below: The perfect place to buy beautiful foods is a beautiful shop. Todd's Vintry on the Pantiles in Tunbridge Wells, Kent is an emporium of delights, in all seasons a place to visit to buy lovely things for yourself or for friends.

Left: Barn shop sign: Countrywide, country lovers with a taste for fine food, set out to tempt the consumer with farm shops filled with a colourful selection of local fare, home grown produce, plants and sometimes even Wellington boots!

The Pantiles show how well fine and specialist food shops can mix with tourist attractions and local custom. A shop called 'Organica' does most of its business with locals, who having discovered a source of fresh organic produce – some 70% of it from local suppliers – use it regularly. Tourists are also attracted by the distinctly modern. fresh interior, the obvious quality of the fruit and vegetables and the offerings of organic cheese and meat.

A countrywide scheme has been launched by the **Rare Breed Survival Trust** to accredit butchers, breeders and finishers of rare breed meats and eggs. Butcher members at the moment are located mainly in England, but it is a continually growing list who wish to offer the public the chance of enjoying the rare meats. An example of this is Hogget lamb, the lamb from some of Britain's rarest breeds. These animals mature slowly, often on poor pasture and need an extra year's growth before they are ready for market. Very different in flavour from mutton – which is

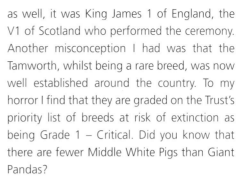

generally from an animal at least three years old, this kind of meat from a breed like the Manx Loghtan – a primitive breed from the Isle of Man – is lean and well flavoured. I always thought that the cut of beef called sirloin earned its name from Henry VIII knighting a particularly fine roast and calling it 'sir loin'. I now gather I was wrong, and that the beef in question actually came from the White Park – the oldest breed of British cattle that was even recorded in Celtic history. I had the wrong king as well, it was King James 1 of England, the V1 of Scotland who performed the ceremony. Another misconception I had was that the Tamworth, whilst being a rare breed, was now well established around the country. To my horror I find that they are graded on the Trust's priority list of breeds at risk of extinction as being Grade 1 – Critical. Did you know that there are fewer Middle White Pigs than Giant Pandas?

It's not only meat that can be enjoyed as part of this positive way of helping conserve rare breeds. There is the distinctive taste of Old English Pheasant Fowl eggs, and the prospect of eating a Double Gloucester cheese, made, as it used to be, with the milk of Gloucester cows, and Wensleydale cheese made with the milk of Wensleydale sheep.

The Rare Breed Survival Trust is very aware that today, in Britain, the buying public wants to know where their food comes from and how it is produced. This desire for knowledge is constanty fuelled by media interest in the food industry. The 'we are what we eat' message is emphasised by scientific research focusing on how diet can effect our health. We expect – quite rightly – our food to be good for us, to be tasty, we also expect to be able to buy what we want to eat when we want it and for it to look tempting and delicious. Our expectations pose many challenges for the food and drink industry.

Facing up to these challenges requires a dedicated, professional approach with an underlying passion for food – and that describes perfectly the many people busily producing '**Great British Food**' today.

Below: A very British habit – starting the day with an egg. Free range for flavour, served with organic bread 'soldiers', thinly spread with butter and sprinkled with finely ground sea salt - eggcellent!

Acknowledgements

The publishers would like to thank the following for the use of their photographs in this book

Agriculture, Department of for Northern Ireland - 128, 129, 131
Alexander, William (the Hop Shop) - 30 (bottom right)
Angel, Heather (Biofotos) - 34
Asparagus Growers Association - 81
Belvoir Fruit Farms - 89
Biddenham Vineyards Ltd (Courtesy of Kent Messenger) - 31, 32
Boathouse Farm - 39
Botterill W.E. - 83
British Deer Farmers Association - 110
British Egg Information Service - 141
Burlington, Bill - 20
Cameron Choat and Partners - 71 (top right)
Carron Lodge Farmhouse, Preston - 112
Cheese Bureau - 142
Corporation of London - 23
Davies, Claire - 5, 12, 19, 27, 44, 45 (top), 48, 49, 52, 61, 70, 79, 86, 92, 102, 122, 138
Denhay Farms Ltd - 55
Dickinson & Morris, Melton Mowbray - 84
English Apples & Pears Ltd - 29
Ffrench Alexander - 3, 4, 7 (right), 8, 9, 10, 16 (bottom), 17, 21, 23, 25, 26, 30 (left), 35 (top), 37 (left), 42, 45 (bottom), 47, 48, 51, 53, 58 (left), 63, 66, 67, 71 (left) 73 (left), 74, 75, 77, 85, 93, 94, 95, 96, 99 (left), 100 (top right), 103, 107, 108 (top), 111, 113, 132, 133 (bottom), 137, 139 (bottom), 140, 144, 148, 149
First Quality Foods, Bristol - 2
Flour Advisory Bureau - 68
Food from Britain - ii, iv, xi, 15, 22, 38, 43, 50, 55, 57, 58 (right), 62, 65, 76, 78, 97, 106, 116 (right), 117 (top), 119, 135, 139 (top)
Fortnum & Mason Plc - 16 (top)
Fresh Fruit & Vegetable Information Bureau - 38
Fundamentally Fungus Ltd - 56
Ginger Pig, The, Tamworth - 87 (left)
Glass House Restaurant, The - 109
Greenwood, A - 100 (bottom)
Hampshire County Council - 6 (left), 87 (right)
Hampshire Fare - 62

Hangland Farm Ostriches - 7
Harrods Ltd - 14
Herefordshire Cattle Breeders Association - 90, 91
Highlands Tourist Board - 114
Hills, Ann - 115
Holmes, Neil - 24, 54, 64, 72, 82, 98, 134
Jordan's Cereals - 136
Lincolnshire County Council - 87 (right)
Loseley Chilled Products Ltd - 35 (bottom)
Manor Cellars, The, A Division of Both Barrels Ltd - 37 (right)
Meat and Livestock Commission -111
Mushroom Bureau - 59, 60
National Summer Fruits Ltd - 40, 41
Northern Ireland Tourist Board -128
Noon, G.K. - 18
Old Bushmills' Distillery Company Limited, The - 133 (top)
Oslink, Boston - 7
Parkview Farm Foods -142
Rare Breeds Survival Trust, The - 108 (bottom)
Sainsbury's Plc - x
Scott, Mark - 39
Scottish Highlands Photo Library - vi, 118, 120, 121, 123, 124, 125, 126
Scottish Highlands Tourist Board - 116 (left), 117 (bottom)
Scottish Whisky Association - 127
Shepherds Gold, Lincolnshire - 151
Shepherds Purse, Thirsk - 99 (right)
Soil Association - 6 (right)
Stilton Cheese Makers' Association - 88
Sunnyside Up - 152
Sussex High Weald Dairy Products - 36, 43
Taste of the South West - 46, 47
Tastes of Anglia - 80
Thaymar Icecream, Repford - 152
Theakstons Brewery - 104
Unigate Plc - vii
Vin Sullivan Foods Ltd, Gwent - 150
Wilkin & Sons Ltd - 73 (right)
Womersley Products - 105
Yorkshire Hills Spring Water Company - 100 (top left), 101

Food and drink speciality groups

A TASTE OF THE SOUTH EAST
(Surrey & Sussex)
Joanna Cummings
Brinsbury College
North Heath
Pulborough
West Sussex RH20 1DL
Tel: 01798 874 250
Fax: 01798 874 256
Email: office@taste-ofthe-southeast.co.uk
www.taste-ofthe-southeast.co.uk

HAMPSHIRE FARE
Henriette Reinders
P.O. Box 211
Winchester
Hampshire SO23 8WB
Tel: 01962 845 999
Fax: 01962 878 131
Email: cxechr@hants.gov.uk
www.hampshirefare.co.uk

HEART OF ENGLAND FINE FOODS
(Herefordshire, Shropshire, Staffordshire, West Midlands, Warwickshire & Worcestershire)
Karen Davies
P.O. Box 1
Much Wenlock
Telford TF13 6WH
Tel: 01746 785 185
Fax: 01746 785 186
Email: office@heff.co.uk
www.heff.co.uk

KENTISH FARE
Rob Weaver
Kent County Council
Invicta House
County Hall
Maidstone
Kent ME14 2LL
Tel: 01622 221 928
Fax: 01622 691 418
Email: robweaver@kent.gov.uk
www.uk-travelguide.co.uk

HIGHLANDS & ISLANDS ENTERPRISE
Kevin Gruer
Bridge House
Bridge Street
Inverness IV1 1QR
Tel: 01463 244 220
Fax: 01463 244 254

MIDDLE ENGLAND FINE FOODS
(Derbyshire, Leicestershire, Lincolnshire, Northamptonshire & Nottinghamshire)
Diana Goodband
3 Kings Farm
Mareham Lane
Threekingham, Sleaford
Lincolnshire NG34 0BQ
Tel: 01529 241 034
Fax: 01529 241 093
Email: office@meff.co.uk
www.meff.co.uk

NORTH WEST FINE FOODS
(Cheshire, Cumbria, Greater Manchester, Lancashire & Merseyside)
Sharon Stopford
The Coach House
Duxbury Hall Road
Duxbury Park
Chorley PR7 4AT
Tel: 01257 226206
Fax: 01257 266687
Email: office@nw-fine-foods.co.uk
Internet: www.nw-fine-foods.co.uk

TASTE OF THE WEST
(Cornwall, Devon, Dorset, Gloucestershire, Somerset & Wiltshire)
Diane Lethbridge
Agriculture House
Pynes Hill
Rydon Lane
Exeter
Devon EX2 5ST
Tel: 01392 440 745
Fax: 01392 440 732
Email: enquiries@tasteofthewest.co.uk
www.devon-cc.gov.uk/taste.of.the.west

TASTES OF ANGLIA
(Bedfordshire, Cambridgeshire, Essex, Hertfordshire, Norfolk & Suffolk)
Jane Whyman
Charity Farmhouse
Otley
Ipswich
Suffolk IP6 9EY
Tel: 01473 785 883
Fax: 01473 785 894
Email: enquiries@tastesofanglia.com
www.tastesofanglia.com

THE YORKSHIRE PANTRY
John Partridge
Economic Development Centre
North Yorkshire County Council
Northallerton
North Yorkshire DL7 8AH
Tel: 01609 780 780
Fax: 01609 779 082
Email: enquiries@yorkshirepantry.co.uk
www.yorkshirepantry.co.uk

A TASTE OF ULSTER
Michelle Bell
c/o DANI
Room 550
Dundonald House
Upper Newtownards Road
Belfast BT4 3SB
Tel: 01232 524 993
Fax: 01232 524 055
Email: michelle.bell@dani.gov.uk

SCOTTISH ENTERPRISE
Jonathan Tait
Food Team
120 Bothwell Street
Glasgow G2 7JP
Tel: 0141 248 2700
Fax: 0141 204 3969
Email: food@scotent.co.uk
www.scottishfoodanddrink.com

WDA FOOD DIRECTORATE
Paul O'Donovan
Cardiff Business Technology Centre
Senghennydd Road
Cardiff CF24 4AY
Tel: 01222 828 986
Fax: 01222 828 998
Email: paul.o'donovan@wda.co.uk

FOOD FROM BRITAIN
Charlotte Lawson
Speciality Foods Director
123 Buckingham Palace Road
London SW1W 9SA
Tel: 0207 233 5111
Fax: 0207 233 9515
Email: clawson@foodfrombritain.co.uk
www.foodfrombritain.com

Homemade Brandy Butter

Sometimes it's the little touches that make all the difference. Making your own brandy butter is as simple as can be, and it means you can use a premium butter like our Netherend Farm Organic. The quality of this is what your homemade Christmas pud or mince pies deserve. Or, if that's a bit beyond your culinary skills, adding it to some you bought gives everything that personal touch.

Ingredients

125g unsalted butter, softened

125g icing sugar

2 tbsp boiling water

3 tbsp brandy

Method

Cream together the butter and the icing sugar.

Beat in the boiling water and brandy until smooth.

Chill until needed and serve with mince pies or Christmas pudding.

Sweet treats

CONFECTIONERY COLLECTION

A **£4.49** COCOA LOCO DARK CHOCOLATE & RASPBERRY STARS
100g

B **£4.49** COCOA LOCO WHITE CHOCOLATE SNOWMEN
110g

C **£6.95** COCOBA DARK CHOCOLATE COVERED BRAZIL NUTS
200g

D **£4.95** COCOBA CHRISTMAS CRACKER WITH MINI BAR AND TWO TRUFFLES

E **£4.95** FLOWER & WHITE CHOCOLATE PRALINE COVERED MERINGUE DROPS
100g

F **£8.99** FLOWER & WHITE MERINGUE TRUFFLES SELECTION
144g

G **£5.50** THE TREAT KITCHEN SWEETS – MILK BOTTLES IN GLASS BOTTLE
310g

H **£5.50** THE TREAT KITCHEN SWEETS – STRAWBERRY BON BONS IN GLASS BOTTLE
340g

I **£5.50** THE TREAT KITCHEN SWEETS – MINI WHITE CHOCOLATE JAZZIES IN GLASS BOTTLE
320g

Distilleries to visit

There are many reasons to tour Scotland, to enjoy the beautiful scenery, to eat the delicious food, and of course to sample the whisky. Scotch whisky, by definition, has to be distilled and matured in Scotland; the best way to appreciate this is to visit some of the many distilleries, for a look at production methods – and a 'wee dram'.

Aberfeldy Distillery
John Dewar & Sons Ltd,
Aberfeldy, Perthshire
01887 822000

Ardbeg Distillery
Glenmorangie plc,
Port Ellen, Isle of Islay
01496 302244

Isle of Arran Distillery
Isle of Arran Distillers Ltd
Lochranza, Isle of Arran
01770 830264

Ben Nevis
Ben Nevis Distillery, (Fort
William) Ltd
Lochy Bridge, Fort William
01397 700400

Blair Athol Distillery
United Distillers & Vintners,
Pitlochry, Perthshire
01796 482003

Bowmore Distillery
Morrison Bowmore Distillers
Ltd
Bowmore, Isle of Islay
01496 810441

Bunnahabhain Distillery
Highland Distillers plc
Port Askaig, Isle of Islay
01496 840646

Caol Ila Distillery
United Distillers & Vintners
Port Askaig, Isle of Islay
01496 302760

Cardhu Distillery
United Distillers & Vintners
Knockando, Aberlour,
Banffshire
01340 872555

Clynelish Distillery
United Distillers & Vintners
Brora, Sutherland
01408 623000

Dalmore Distillery
UBB (Greater Europe) plc
Alness, Ross-shire
01349 882362

Dalwhinnie Distillery
United Distillers & Vintners
Dalwhinnie, Inverness-shire
01528 522208

Edradour Distillery
Campbell Distillers Ltd
Pitlochry, Perthshire
01796 472095

Fettercairn Distillery
JBB (Greater Europe) plc
Fettercairn, Laurencekirk,
Kincardineshire
01561 340205

Glencadam Distillery
Allied Distillers Ltd
Brechin, Angus
01356 622217

The Glendronach Distillery
Allied Distillers Ltd
Forgue by Huntly,
Aberdeenshire
01466 730202

Glenfarclas Distillery
J&G Grant
Ballindalloch, Banfshire
01807 500257

Glenfiddich Distillery
William Grant & Sons Ltd
Dufftown, Banfshire
01340 820373

Glengoyne Distillery
The Edrington Group
Dumgoyne, Nr Killearn,
Stirlingshire
01360 550254

Glen Grant Distillery
Chivas Brothers Ltd
Rothes, Morayshire
01542 783318

Glenkinchie Distillery
United Distillers & Vintners
Pencaitland, East Lothian
01875 342004

The Glenlivet Distillery
Chivas Brothers Ltd
Glenlivet, Ballindalloch,
Banffshire
01542 783220

Glenmorangie Distillery
Tain, Ross-shire
01862 892477

Glen Moray Distillery
Glenmorangie plc
Bruceland Road
Elgin, Morayshire
01343 542577

Glen Ord Distillery
United Distillers & Vintners
Muir of Ord, Ross-shire
01463 872004

Glenturret Distillery
Highland Distillers plc
The Hosh, Crief, Perthshire
01764 656565

Highland Park Distillery
Highland Distillers plc
Holm Road, Kirkwall, Orkney
01856 874619

Isle of Jura Distillery
JBB (Greater Europe) plc
Craighouse, Isle of Jura
01496 820240

Lagavulin Distillery
United Distillers & Vintners
Port Ellen, Isle of Islay
01496 302400

Laphroaig Distillery
Allied Distillers Ltd
Port Ellen, Isle of Islay
01496 302418

The Macallan Distillery
Highland Distillers Ltd
Craigellachie, Banffshire
01340 871471

Miltonduff-Glenlivet Distillery
Allied Distillers Ltd
Elgin, Morayshire
01343 547433

Oban Distillery
United Distillers & Vitners
Oban, Argyllshire
01631 572004

Royal Lochnagar Distillery
United Distillers & Vintners
Crathie, Ballater
01339 742273

Strathisla Distillery
Chivas Bothers Ltd
Seafield Avenue, Keith,
Banffshire
01542 783044

Talisker Distillery
United Distillers & Vintners
Carbost, Isle of Skye
01478 640314

Tobermory Distillery
Burn Stewart Distillers plc
Tobermory. Isle of Mull
01688 302645

Tomatin Distillery
Tomatin Distillery Co Ltd
Tomatin, Inverness-shire
01808 511444

The Tomintoul-Speyside
Distillery
JBB (Greater Europe) plc
Ballindalloch, Banffshire
01807 590274

The Tormore Distillery
Allied Distillers Ltd
Advie, Grantown-on-Spey,
Morayshire
01807 510244

Vineyards to visit

Part of the pleasure in getting to know English wine is to visit the places it is made, and see the grapes it comes from. Winemakers tend to be enthusiastic and delight in talking about their products over a tasting. All of the following welcome visitors, some are open 7 days a week, and some by appointment only so it's worth a phone call before you go.

Kent

Barnsole Vineyard
Fleming Road
Staple
Canterbury
01304 812530

Bearsted Vineyard
Carling Lane
Bearsted
Maidstone
01622 736974

Biddenden Vineyard
Gribble Bridge Lane
Biddenden
01580 291726

Chapeldown Wines
Spots Farm
Smallhythe
Tenterden
01580 763033

Conghurst Vineyard
Conghurst Lane
Hawkhurst
Kent
01580 752634

Groombridge Place
Groombridge
01892 861444

Harbourne Vineyard
Wittersham
Tenterden
01797 270420

Leeds Castle
Maidstone
01622 765400

Pembury Vineyard
Pippins Farm
Pembury
01892 824544

Penshurst Vineyards
Grove Road
Penshurst
01892 870255

Rowenden Vineyard
Sandhurst Lane
Rolvenden
Cranbrook
01580 241255

Staple Vineyard
Church Farm
Staple
Canterbury
01304 812571

Tenterden Vineyard
Small Hythe
Tenterden
01580 763033

Throwley Vineyard
Throwley
Faversham
01795 890276

South East

Denbies Wine Estate
London Road
Dorking
Surrey
01306 876616

Thorncroft Vineyard
Thorncroft Drive
Leatherhead
Surrey
01372 372406

Bookers Vineyard
Foxhole Lane
Bolney
West Sussex
01444 881575

Chanctonbury Vineyard
North Lane
Wiston
West Sussex
01903 892721

Lurgashall Winery
Lurgashall
Petworth
West Sussex
01428 707292

Nutbourne Vineyards
Gay Street
Nr Pulborough West Sussex
01798 815196

Nyetimber Vineyard
West Chillington
West Sussex
01798 813989

Barkham Manor Vineyard
Piltdown
Nr Uckfield
East Sussex
01825 722103

Breaky Bottom Vineyard
Rodmell
Lewes
East Sussex
01273 476427

Carr Taylor Vineyards
Westfield
Hastings
East Sussex
01424 752501

Davenport Vineyards
Limney Farm
Castle Hill
Rotherfield
East Sussex
01892 852380

The English Wine Centre
Alfriston Roundabout
East Sussex
01323 870164

Hidden Spring Vineyard
Vines Cross Road
Horam
Nr Heathfield
East Sussex
01435 812640

Leeford Wines, Battle Wine Estate
Whatlington
Battle
East Sussex
01424 773183

Methersham Vineyard
Hobbs Lane
Beckley
Rye
East Sussex
01797 260621

Plumpton College
Ditchling Road
Plumpton
Nr Lewes
East Sussex
01273 890454

Ridgeview Wine Estate
Fragbarrow Lane
Ditchling Common
East Sussex
01444 241441

Wessex

Northbrook Springs Vineyard
Beeches Hill
Bishops Waltham
Southampton
01489 892659

Horton Estate Vineyard
Horton
Wimborne
Dorset
01258 840258

Beaulieu Vineyard
Beaulieu
Brockenhurst
Hampshire
01590 612345

Rosemary Vineyard
Rosemary Lane
Ryde
Isle of Wight
01983 811084

Wickham Vineyard
Botley Road
Shedfield
Southampton
01329 834042

Marlings Vineyard
Mead End Road
Sway
Hampshire
01590 682256

East Anglia

Bardfield Vineyard
Great Bardfield
Essex
01371 810776

Boyton Vineyard
Boyton End
Stoke-by-Clare
Suffolk
01440 761893

Bruisyard Vineyard
Bruisyard
Saxmundham
Suffolk
01728 638281

Carters Vineyards
Green Lane
Boxted
Colchester
01206 271136

Chilford Hundred Vineyard
Chilford Hall
Linton
Cambridge
01223 892641

Coton Orchards
Cambridge Road
Coton Cambs
01954 210234

Felsted Vineyard
Crix Green
Felsted
Essex
01245 361504

Gifford's Hall Vineyard
Hartest
Nr Bury St Edmunds
Suffolk
01284 830464

Great Stocks Vineyard
Stock
Ingatestone
Essex
01277 841122

Harling Vineyards
East Harling
Norfolk
01953 717341

Helions Vineyard
Helions
Bumpstead
Essex
01440 730316

Howe Green House Vineyard
How Green
Hertford
01707 261377

Ickworth Vineyard
Horringer
Bury St Edmunds
Suffolk
01359 251173

Mersea Vineyard
Rewsalls Lane
East Mersea
Essex
01206 385900

New Hall Vineyard
Purleigh
Chelmsford
Essex
01621 828343

Nevards Vineyard
Boxted
Nr Colchester
Essex
01728 648471

Oakhill Vineyard
Fressingfield
Nr Eye
Suffolk
01379 586455

Sascombe Vineyards
Kirtling
Nr Newmarket
Suffolk
01440 783100

Shawsgate Vineyard
Framlington
Woodbridge
Suffolk
01728 724060

Wyken Vineyards
Stanton
Bury St Edmunds
Suffolk
01359 250287

West of England and Wales

Brecon Court Vineyard
Llansoy
Nr Usk
Gwent
Wales
01291 650366

Camel Valley Vineyard
Nanstallon Bodmin
Cornwall
01208 77959

Coddington Vineyard
Coddington
Nr Ledbury
Herefordshire
01531 640668

Cwm Deri Vineyard
Martletwy
Pembrokeshire
Wales
01834 891274

Down St Mary Vineyard
Down St Mary
Nr Crediton
Devon
01363 823000

Elms Cross Vineyard
Bradford-on-Avon
Wiltshire
01225 866917

Frome Vally Vineyard
Paunton Court
Bishops Frome
Herefordshire
01885 490735

Ffynnon Las Vineyard
Lampter Road
Aberaeron
Dyfed
Wales
01545 570234

Little Ashley Vineyard
Bradford on Avon

Wiltshire
01225 867616

Llanerch Vineyard
Pendoyland
Vale of Glamorgan
Wales
01443 225877

Manstree Vineyard
Shillingford St George
Exeter
Devon
01392 832218

Moorlynch Vineyard
Moorlinch
Nr Bridgewater
Somerset
01458 210393

Mumfords Vineyard
Bannerdown
Bath
01225 858367

Oakford Vineyard
Oakford
Tiverton
Devon
01398 351486

Oatley Vineyard
Cannington
Bridgewater
Somerset
01278 671340

Offa's Vineyard
Llanvihangel-Y-Llewern
Monmouth
Wales
01600 780241

Pemboa Vineyard
Helston
Cornwall
01326 563116

St Anne's Vineyard
Oxenhall
Nr Newent
Gloucestershire
01989 720313

St Augustine's Vineyard
Aust,
South Gloucestershire
01454 632236

St Sampson Vineyard
Golant by Fowey
Cornwall
01726 833707

Sharpham Vineyard
Ashprington
Totnes
Devon
01803 732203

South Beara Vineyard
Chulmleigh
Devon
01769 580726

Staplecombe Vineyards
Staplegrove
Taunton
Somerset
01823 451217

Sugarloaf Vineyard
Pentre Lane
Abergavenny
Wales
01873 858675

Three Choirs Vineyard
Newent
Gloucestershire
01531 890223

Tiltridge Vineyard
Upton-on-Severn
Worcestershire
01684 592906

Veryan Vineyard
Portloe
Nr Truro
Cornwall
01872 501404

Yearlstone Vineyard
Bickleigh
Tiverton
Devon
01884 855700

The Midlands and North of England

Astley Vineyards
Astley
Stourport-on-Severn
Worcester
01299 822907

Chevelswarde Vineyard
South Kilworth
Lutterworth
Leicesteshire
01858 575309

Eglantine Vineyard
Costock
Loughborough
Leicestershire
01509 852386

Hagley Court Vineyard
Bartestree
Hereford
01432 850003

Halfpenny Green Vineyard
Bobbington
Stourbridge
Staffordshire
01384 221122

Leventhorpe Vineyard
Woodlesford
Leeds
0113 288 9088

Mount Pleasant Vineyard
Bolton-le-Sands
Carnforth
Lancashire
01524 732038

Welland Valley Vineyard
Marston Trussell
Market Harborough
Leicestershire

Windmill Vineyard
Hellidon
Northamptonshire
01327 262023

Worthenbury Wines
Worthenbury
Wrexham
01948 770257

Wroxeter Roman Vineyard
Wroxeter
Shrewsbury
Shropshire
01743 761888

Personal suggestions of where to eat, shop and visit

Right: Pearly King and Queen. The pattern on their clothes is handed down through the generations, as is their tradition of raising money for charity and preserving some of the atmosphere of the Old East End.

London:

Places to visit:
The Banqueting House (Historic Royal Palaces Agency)
Whitehall
0207 839 7569
Designed by Inigo Jones for James I (of England) and VIth (of Scotland)

Queen Charlotte's Cottage
(Historic Royal Palaces Agency)
Kew
Used by the family of King George III for picnics, entry via Kew Gardens

A week in the Capital of Food

Day 1 - Made a start at the Sugar Club, Nottinghill for inspiring, award winning Pacific Rim dishes to pep up the digestion for the week ahead.

Day 2 - On to a little light Conran, at Sartoria in Saville Row for English classics with a touch of Italian in a serious style venue (rather like the neighbouring tailors!)

Day 3 - Lured by the prospect of more Italian, a visit to Assaggi, a 'village' trattoria above a pub in Chepstow Place, for dishes like Mamma – on her very best day – used to cook.

Above: Take-away with a difference! More East End tradition, pie and mash, untraditionally sold from a catering trailer, but still with lots of steaming gravy.

Day 4 - Surfeit requires exercise and tempting Tapas, a gentle meander to The Rock in Fulham Road, salted almonds to begin with please...

Day 5 - A change of scene and a black cab to Hackney where appetite is reawakened by corriander and sweet basil scented Vietnamese cooking at Miss Saigon in Kingsland Road.

Day 6 - A sudden fancy for the Great British Breakfast, enjoyed at the organic Café in Lonsdale Road, Willesden, enjoyed, since it's lunchtime, rather decadently with a glass of organic wine.

Day 7 - Back into the heart of town to the River Restaurant at the Savoy in The Strand for a finale of British produce at its best – to start with wild salmon, to finish fresh strawberries - and in between? so hard to choose; I might just have to come back next week...

You can have weeks and weeks like this, armed with nothing more than a credit card and an A-Z to find your way around. From one nation's cooking to another, and everywhere people with opinions on the food, the style, the quality, the price - London, the edible world in microcosm - enjoy!

Kent:

Places to shop:
The Barnyard
Gore Farm
Upchurch
01634 235059
Focus on top quality seasonal produce in lovely old barn brought all the way from Hereford

The Hop Shop
Castle Farm
Shoreham
01959 523219
Stunning home - grown dried flowers and herbs

Macknade Farm Shop
Selling Road
Faversham
01795 534497
Emporium of fresh and preserved local, national and Italian produce

Perry Court Farm Shop
Bilting
01223 812408
Freshly picked fruit and vegetables. Good range of regional cheese

Warren Farm Shop
New Romney
01797 363837
Superb quality home farm meat and regional produce

Places to eat:
The Chafford Arms
Fordcombe
01892 740267
Award winning garden, log fire, and excellent fish dishes

Above: A basket weaver and (opposite below) his creations.

Right: Sales of wares from Plaw Hatch.

The Crown Inn
Sarre
01843 847914
Local fruit, lamb and oysters,
Shepherd Neame ales

Places to visit:
Knole (National Trust)
Sevenoaks
Magnificent 15th century house in
splendid Park with many mature,
fruiting, chestnuts.

Rochester Castle Keep (National
Trust)
Rochester
11th century Norman Castle, close to
the High Street where pre Christmas
festivities feature mulled wine, mince
pies and Chinese food being cooked
outdoors.

South East:

Places to shop:
Tulley's Farm
Turners Hill
West Sussex
01342 718472
Farm shop, PYO and very good
farmhouse - kitchen restaurant

The English Wine Centre
Alfriston
East Sussex
01323 870164
Dozens of different English wines and
tutored tastings

Places to eat:
The Avins Bridge Restaurant and
Rooms
College Road
Ardingly
West Sussex
01444 892393
Lots of local food imaginatively
cooked

Botley Hill Farmhouse Public House
Warlingham
Surrey

01959 577154
Award winning inn, all food freshly
prepared

Places to visit:
Bateman's (National Trust)
Nr Burwash
Sussex
Home of Rudyard Kipling, beautiful
17th century house and working mill
- the stoneground flour is excellent

Petworth House (National Trust)
Petworth
West Sussex
Magnificent 17th century house with
deer park, where Turner painted.
Original kitchens on view.

West Country:

Places to shop:
The Pantry by the Pond
Castle Cary
Somerset
01963 351777

Pavey's Delicatessen
New Street
Honiton
Devon
01404 42589

Places to eat:
The White Hart
Ford
Chippenham
Wiltshire
01249 782213
Award winning 16th centurry
riverside inn

The Carved Angel
South Embankment
Dartmouth
Devon
Fantastic setting and food

Places to visit
Avebury Museum
Avebury
Wiltshire

Prehistoric archaeological collection,
much of it donated by the Keiller
family - of marmalade fame

A la Ronde
Exmouth
Devon
Intriguing 16 sided house with
fantastic shell decorated gallery and
stunning views, excellent food in the
old kitchens

Hampshire:

Places to shop:
Beaulieu Chocolates
Beaulieu
01590 612279
Luxurious handmade chocolates and
local wines

Linzi's Patisserie
Lymington
01590 678980
14 different varieties of fruitcake -
and more

Right: Organic Vegetables in the farm shop.

Places to eat:
Chewton Glen Hotel
New Milton
01425 275341
Michelin star and superb health/sporting facilities

Terracotta Room
Wickham Vineyard
Shedfield
01329 835454
Australian style with local ingredients

Places to visit:
Hinton Ampner
Alresford
Glorious scented gardens

Winchester City Mill
Winchester
Dating from 1744, a reminder of how important flour and bread have always been in British food

Below: A gamey cornucopia from Vin Sullivan of Gwent.

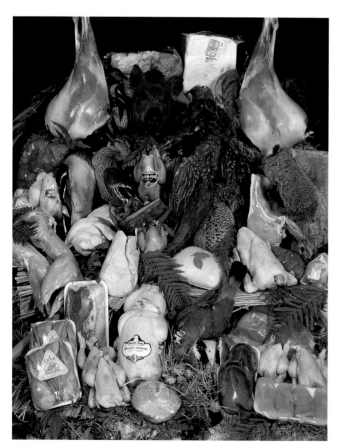

Wales:

Places to shop:
Welsh Mountain Garden Hotel
Maes-y-Neuadd
Harlech
Gwynedd
01766 780319
All kinds of beautifully presented preserves using produce of the kitchen garden and surrounding hedgerows - you can eat, and stay, here as well - what nicer way to shop?

Rhydlewis Trout Farm and Smokery
Rhydlewis,
Llandysul
Dyfed
01239 851224
Trout, fresh and smoked, also smoked salmon, speciality fish and smoked cheese

Places to eat:
The Griffin Inn
Llyswen nr Brecon
01874 754241
Beautifully situated in the Upper Wye Valley, famous for its deliciously Welsh cooking and very popular – ring to book

Gliffaes Country House Hotel
Crickhowell
Powys
01874 730371
Beautiful food, and the hotel owns a 2.5 mile stretch of the River Usk, famous for its trout and salmon

Places to visit:
Cilgerran Castle
Cilgerran
Nr Cardigan
Dating from the 13th century, perched above a deep gorge, perfect for picnics

Caerphilly Castle
Caerphilly
One of the largest surviving Western medieval castles

Anglia:

Places to shop:
Say Cheese
Sheringham
Norfolk
01328 856161
Over 120 cheeses on display

Friday Street Farm Shop
Saxmundham
Suffolk
01728 602783
Locally grown fruit and vegetables, goats milk, preserves, etc

Places to eat:
Redcoats Farmhouse Hotel and Restaurant
Redcoats Green
Nr Hitchin
Hertfordshire
Superb choice of dishes

The Swan Hotel
Southwold
Suffolk
01502 727260
Owned by Adnams Brewery, inevitably the beer is first rate as is the food and comfort

Places to visit:
Berney Arms Windmill
Reedham
Norfolk
Marsh windmill on seven floors

Above: Sheep for milking from Shepherd's Gold, Lincolnshire.

Peckover House and Garden
Wisbech
Cambs
Victorian garden and interesting early-18th-century house

Middle England:

Places to eat:
Burford House Gardens Tea Rooms
Tenbury Wells
Worcestershire
WR15 8HQ
01684 810777

The Riverside Inn and Restaurant
Aymestry
Herefordshire
HR6 9ST
01668 708440

Bird in Hand
Newbold-on-Stour
Warwickshire
01789 450253
Home smoked trout, local game and eggs from the publican's bantam hens, a real country pud.

Places to visit:
Sibsey Trader Windmill (English Heritage)
Sibsey
Lincolnshire
Tower mill with six sails, built in 1877, still milling.

Stokesay Castle (English Heritage)
Ludlow
13th century fortified manor house

Heart of England:

Places to eat:
Penrhos Court
Kington
Hereford
01544 230720
Beautiful, timbered dining hall
Organic food with flair.

Old Coach House
Ashby St. Ledgers
Northamptonshire
01788 890349
An enthusiastic 'real ale' pub. With their own brew and imaginative food such as Old Hooky Pie.

The Olde Stocks Restaurant
Main Street
Grimston
Nr. Melton Mowbray
Leicestershire
LE14 3BZ
Contact Penni & Jack Harrison
01664 812255

Hambleton Hall
Hambleton
Oakham
Rutland
LE15 8TH
Contact Tim Hart
01572 756991

Places to visit:
The Weir
Swainshill
Herefordshire
Delightful garden with views of the river Wye, close to the town of Hereford, source of excellent local produce

Shugborough
near Stafford
Fine house in magnificent parkland, Seat of Earl of Lichfield

Yorkshire:

Places to shop:
Lewis and Cooper
High Street
Northallerton
01609 772880
Wide range of Yorkshire fare including exclusive plum puddings

Places to eat
Mallyan Spout Hotel
Goathland
Whitby
01947 896486
On North York Moors with good home cooking

Charles' Bistro
Market Place
Thirsk
01845 527444
Yorkshire produce, mediterranean style

Places to visit:
Scarborough Castle
Scarborough
In a spectacular coastal position, the ruins of a 12th century castle

Merchant Adventurers' Hall
York
One of Europe's finest Guild Halls

Thaymar icecream from Nottinghamshire.

Happy hens from Sunnyside Up, Lincolnshire.

North West:

Places to shop:
James & John Graham
Market Square
Penrith
Cumbria
01768 862281

Country Harvest
Ingleton
Via Carnworth
Lancashire

Places to eat:
The Village Bakery (licensed restaurant)
Melmbery
Cumbria
01768 881515

Low Sizergh Barn Farmshop, Tea Room & Craft Gallery
Kendal
Cumbria
015395 60426
Enjoy fresh, local produce and watch the milking through the viewing window

Places to visit:
Hill Top
Nr Sawrey
Where Beatrix Potter wrote many of her stories

Dove Cottage & The Wordsworth Museum
Grasmere
Wordsworth's home from 1799 to 1808

Scotland:

Places to shop:
Glasgow is full of exciting places to shop, try Sauchiehall Street and Argyle Street for a bustling feel of the City, and for even more crowds, Paddy's Market, by Clyde Street

Visit Edinburgh and you are drawn by the magnet that is Princes Street, perhaps it's because of the nearby volcanic 'plug' topped by Edinburgh Castle, or perhaps it's the shops. Finish with a look at the floral clock in Princes Street Gardens for a taste of the city

Places to eat:
Peebles Hydro Hotel
Peebles
0721 20602
Apart from excellent food, this chateau-style
Border hotel offers wonderful views of the Tweed

L'Auberge
St. Mary's Street
Edinburgh
031556 5888
French-style cooking of fresh Scottish produce

Places to visit:
Edinburgh Castle
Edinburgh
World famous ancient fortress built on rock, walk down to Princes Street to buy the almost as famous sweet, Edinburgh Rock

Black House
Arnol
Isle of Lewis
Furnished Lewis thatched house with echoes of a simpler life

Northern Ireland:

Places to shop:
McCartney's Family Butchers
Main Street,
Moira
County Down
01846 611422
Established over 100 years, focus on Ulster meat, including over 30 varieties of sausages

Something to buy:
Saint Brendan's Irish Cream Liqueur
01504 343434
Irish whisky and fresh dairy cream - sounds as good as it tastes!

Places to eat:
McGilloways Seafood Restaurant
Strand Road
Derry City
01504 262050
Wide selection of locally cooked fish, lots of delicious sauces

The Lobster Pot
The Square
Strangford
01396 881288
Marvellous lobster, Irish and European dishes using fresh local produce

Places to visit:
Wellbrook Beetling Mill
Cookstown
County Tyrone
Early water-powered mill for manufacturing linen

Ardress House
Portadown
County Armagh
17th-century country house with livestock display

Index of speciality foods